# Finding Our Story

# Finding
## Our
# Story

## Narrative Leadership
## and Congregational Change

~

Larry A. Golemon, Editor

THE
ALBAN
INSTITUTE
Herndon, Virginia
www.alban.org

The Alban Institute
2121 Cooperative Way, Suite 100
Herndon, VA 20171

Scripture quotations, unless otherwise noted, are from the New Revised Standard Version of the Bible, copyright © 1989, Division of Christian Education of the National Council of Churches of Christ in the United States of America, and are used by permission.

The excerpt on page 27 is from *The Story Factor* by Annette Simmons (New York: Basic Books, 2001), 27, copyright © 2001 by Annette Simmons. Reprinted by permission of BASIC BOOKS, a member of Perseus Books Group.

Cover design by Spark Design.

Library of Congress Cataloging-in-Publication Data

Finding our story : narrative leadership and congregational change / Larry A. Golemon, editor.
    p. cm.
    Includes bibliographical references.
    ISBN 978-1-56699-376-0
    1. Narrative theology. 2. Storytelling--Religious aspects--Christianity. 3. Christian leadership. 4. Change (Psychology)--Religious aspects--Christianity. 5. Religious gatherings--Christianity. I. Golemon, Larry A.
    BT83.78.F56 2009
    254'.501--dc22
                        2009037981

10   11   12   13   14   VP   5   4   3   2   1

# Contents

121247

# Preface

～

Congregations in America are often victims of larger narratives they inherit. Old mainline Protestants have been swept up in disestablishment narratives and loss of market share since the Revolutionary days. Catholic parishes have been defined by stories of European ethnicity and American inculturation since their founding. Evangelical churches have been caught in the wake of the fundamentalist-modernist divide of the early twentieth century. And Jewish congregations have taken positions in different versions of *halakich* reform and support for Zion since their founding. Add to these American religious legacies the increased competition with the global market, rising religious pluralism, radical secularization, and competition with the culture industry for worship time and space, and American congregations are bombarded with multiple narratives that sometimes appear to control their destiny.

The Alban Institute has years of experience working with local congregations to recover healthy practices that open a viable, sustainable future. Recently, Alban began to look at various kinds of narrative work in churches and synagogues that overcome disabling stories, from without and within, and help create a new direction. With funding from the Luce Foundation, Alban began consultations, congregational visitations, and literature reviews to explore how generative narrative work was being done in healthy, vibrant congregations. In addition, Alban consultants began to focus more on narrative work in their own practices by tracking how congregations can overcome disabling stories, and how pastors, priests, rabbis, and other leaders can work with congregations and parishes to generate new stories of promise. This book shares some of their findings, and it is the first of three that are part of the Alban Institute's Narrative Leadership series.

I open this book with an overview of narrative theory and practice in various fields that will help congregational leaders focus on the nature and means of constructive change. I begin with an appreciation of the legacy of James Hopewell, who brought narrative analysis to the field of congregational studies and is especially helpful in identifying the cultural myths and genres that often paralyze congregations into fixed ways of thinking—usually around tragedy, comedy, romance, or irony. Then I explore how narrative work has evolved in the fields of congregational studies, religious practice, and practical theology in order to find practical tools that leaders might use to do constructive narrative work in their own congregations. I find the work of Diana Butler Bass especially helpful for churches seeking to construct a new narrative that is grounded in healthy congregational practices. I next outline aspects of narrative work in family systems, narrative therapy, and business models of narrative change that can help congregational leaders. While other authors in this volume highlight the value of narrative therapy, I end by focusing on the contributions of Stephen Denning in story-based models of change in business.

In chapter 2, Gil Rendle, who was instrumental in helping Alban begin its work in narrative leadership, focuses on the nature of powerful, generative narratives. He offers two examples—one from a Methodist, urban pastor, the other from Denning's "springboard stories" in business. Then he explores the power of narrative to elicit intuitive wisdom and response in ways that facts, figures, and rational appeals cannot. Rendle finds that most of the congregations he works with stick to stories about themselves that are either too weak (by drawing on forgotten legacies) or too safe (by avoiding risk or trying not to offend). To remedy this, he combines a paradigm from group dialogue and from organizational development to identify four key phases of good narrative leadership: politeness and forming, breakdown and storming, inquiry and norming, flow and performing. This model identifies patterns of gathering, deconstructing, inquiry, and reconstructing healthy church narratives and practices that help build a new congregational identity. Rendle's experienced wisdom and passion for congregational change will challenge any leader.

Chapter 3, by Alban consultant Larry Peers, begins with the difference between telling a good story and a story as a way of being. By drawing on Howard Gardner's work on exemplary narrative leaders, Peers challenges congregational leaders to embody the narrative they find most helpful for their community. He uses Hopewell's work to challenge leaders to identify the kind of story they tell about their congregation—be it one of a lack of commitment, resources, or fervor—and to ask how we as leaders contribute to the problem-based stories our congregations are stuck in. Peers asks leaders to shift their inner story about ministry by attending carefully to the internal dialogue we experience around their work. Then he shares a model adapted from the narrative therapy work of Michael White and David Epston that guides leaders and congregations in several phases of changing a congregation's story: unpacking the problem-saturated story; depersonalizing the problem by externalizing it; and constructing a new, more promising narrative together. Throughout the essay, Peers draws on congregational examples and scriptural accounts that enflesh his framework.

Alice Mann offers us a glimpse of her new work on "place-based narratives" in chapter 4. As a long-time Alban consultant, Mann shares her conviction that congregations—like people—need to find their home in the place where they have landed. Due to a rapidly changing economy, demographic mobility, and shifts in urban-rural landscapes, congregations and local communities need a renewed sense of place to revitalize their stories of origin, identity, and purpose. As Mann explains, place-based narratives are a "powerful component of personal, civic, and congregational life" because they identify the boundaries, history, future, and shared concerns that make up the "soul of a community." Mann draws on John Paul Lederach's work in conflict transformation to describe how a "local fabric of relationships" is embodied in a community's sense and narrative of place. She offers a remarkable review of categories from congregational and community studies that helps congregations expand their vocabulary about place: including being a parish or a commuter congregation; specializing in bonding (inner) or bridging (community-based) social capital; being a sanctuary, evangelistic, civic, or activist congregation, and more. Mann shares a process that helps congregations ask soul-searching questions, like "What have we been to this place?" and "What is God's call to us today?" In the end, she offers a powerful example from her own community of a local narrative that is being contested and redefined, and she describes a community-wide process that involves local congregations and civic groups in that process. Mann's essay is filled with years of experience, a vast range of literature, and a deep passion for her own community and place.

The fifth chapter, by Alban consultant Susan Beaumont, begins with a creative Midrash on the accounts of the Promised Land in Numbers 13 that focus on giants and grasshoppers instead of milk and honey. Beaumont reflects on congregations that are paralyzed by anxiety as they cope with the bombardment of narratives around them: from multicultural dynamics to worship wars. Drawing on Peter Steinke's work in family systems, she shares how anxious congregations shape stories that "frame and contain their angst," and she explores three types of stuck stories with examples from her work. The first kind of story tells of a wrong turn in the past that cannot be recovered from—here illustrated by a church that "split" members and resources when in reality it was birthing a mission parish. Another kind memorializes a triumphant moment in ways that limit present action—retold in one congregation's memory of a devoted laywoman who kept the church doors open for years without a pastor, forgetting that she voted to raze the building when a new pastor came. A third kind of stuck story tells of a present conflict by enobling some actors and blaming others, which is typified by a church that claims it is in conflict with a new pastor's theology, while it overlooks feeling uncared for around pastoral issues. Beaumont concludes by sharing concrete processes of careful listening and community storytelling that can help congregations reframe their "stuck" stories and move toward a new narrative shaped by core values and unencumbered by organizational obstacles. Beaumont's creativity and energetic description provide readers ways to find their own congregations in the mix.

Next, in chapter 6, Alban consultant Susan Nienaber writes on the power of shaping narratives around congregational resilience, especially for times of crisis. She draws on the narrative theory of White and Epston to describe how congregations can overcome problem narratives, identify strengths and resiliencies, and forge new narratives of hope. Through her own experience and love of gardening, Nienaber reflects on the ways that narratives are constructed by us in relation with others to shape individual and collective identity. She examines with sensitivity how communities are filled with multivalent, sometimes conflicting narratives, which are constantly being negotiated. Nienaber is aware of the dynamics of social pluralism and change that put narratives into competition with each other. She focuses in her work on listening for the ways that congregations faced change or conflict in their past, primarily by drawing on their strengths of resilience. She sums up a process that helps resilient congregations revisit and reframe their stories: including deconstructing old stories to clear up communication, asking lots of questions, externalizing a problem, listening for exceptions and naming alternative story-lines, and remembering the past in ways that support growth and change. She explores practical techniques of using video and print to extend the conversation and to celebrate discoveries through shared ritual and gatherings. With postmodern sensitivity and insight, Nienaber's essay offers congregations ways to find and build upon their lasting strengths.

These essays bring together the insights from some of the finest consultants Alban has known to bear on the narrative work of congregational change. As the world changes exponentially, and new narratives seek to drown out or paralyze those we inherited, I trust every congregational leader will find tools, frameworks, and strategies for helping churches and synagogues forge more viable narratives of purpose and identity for the future.

Larry A. Golemon
Director
The Alban Institute Narrative Leadership Project

# CHAPTER I

# Thinking through Change
## NARRATIVE THEORY AND
## MODELS OF TRANSFORMATION

⁓

### LARRY A. GOLEMON

Many essays in this volume combine the practical wisdom of experienced congregational consultants with a favorite model of change the consultant has found most helpful in his or her work. Various models have been tapped in these consultants' work, including ones from counseling, psychology, business, and place-based literature. In this first essay, I will share various models of change that the project leaders have explored during the Alban Institute's project on Narrative Leadership, and offer them to congregational leaders, consultants, and judicatory staff who seek new ways to think about change in the congregations and institutions they serve.

I will begin by exploring how narrative methods in *congregational studies* and the research in *congregational practices* identify the dynamics of and prospects for change for church and synagogue. Then I explore approaches to *systems change* in narrative therapy and a business model of adaptive leadership.

# Narrative Approaches
# in Congregational Studies

Congregational studies is a field within theological education that combines methods of sociology, anthropology, management theory, and practical theology to understand the culture, social dynamics, and ministry of local congregations. While this field arose out of early efforts to apply human relations and organizational management theory to the local church— including the work of Loren Mead and others at the Alban Institute—it came into its own in the theological school by early founders of the field like James Hopewell, author of the seminal work *Congregations: Stories and Structure*. Here, I want to explore Hopewell's legacy in today's environment of congregational studies and practical theology, with a distinct focus on the value of his narrative approach to theories of change for congregations.

Hopewell's legacy lies primarily in how to develop a "thick description" of each congregation's uniqueness through narrative means. But his framework does have direct implications for a model of change. To understand a congregation, a pastor or researcher must uncover the rich, metaphorical nature of a congregation's imagination. To do so, the common language and marker events of a congregation must be reframed by means of the core myths at work—myths drawn largely from human experience and culture. To illuminate the narrative imagination of a church or synagogue, Hopewell draws upon the literary typology of Northrop Frye, which organizes cultural myths in relation to two axes: the tragic-comic pole and the romantic-ironic pole. Congregations usually operate out of a worldview that is defined by its place on these axes:

Tragic worldview: a hero-centered drama of promise, struggle, and failure that forces a community back on an au-
thoritative, *canonic* interpretation of divine will

Comic worldview: people are certain everything will work
out, based upon an intuitive, *gnostic* sense of hidden
harmony that they must discover

Romantic worldview: trust in supernatural happenings
communicated by a *charismatic* personality, who is often pitted against the facts of reality or an antagonist,
and the struggle ends in triumph

Ironic worldview: accepting reality as it is in all its contra-
dictions, reliance on *empirical*, verifiable data instead of
miracles, heroic figures, or hidden realities

Hopewell prefers the italicized terminology above for a congregation's worldview—canonic, gnostic, charismatic, empiric.
These worldviews are culturally formed, and often determine
the way the gospel or Christ story is understood so that a congregation's way of relating the faith is equated with the gospel
itself.

There are two implications for change in Hopewell's view.
First, a congregation's way of articulating its life must be reen-
coded in mythic or metaphorical terms from the larger culture.
Hopewell, in fact, identifies a "core myth" in each congregation
that identifies its handling of the most important recent events
of transition, loss, or change. In a study of Wiltshire Church,
for example, he identifies a "*chronos* myth" whereby the new,
transformative pastor acts like Zeus who has to slay the old
order of the previous pastor to bring about a new era of growth
and prosperity. This struggle fulfills a *charismatic* or romantic
worldview in this church. The working myth of a congregation
need not be from classical mythology (Hopewell's usual preference); rather, it is important to remythologize the imagination
and worldview of a church in relation to core narratives of the

surrounding culture (presumably possible from movies, sports superstars, or even comic book characters).

The second implication for change is that a congregation must be asked if its working myth is consonant with its understanding of the gospel, or we might add the Torah. Hopewell articulates a tension between "Eros and Christos" myths in Christian congregations—the former drawn from culture and the latter from the Scriptures and Christian tradition. Yet the local mixing of the two—which Hopewell usually sees as inextricably linked—implies that they could enter a critical relation, toward eventual separation. Might a church caught in a decade-long cycle of blaming and expelling pastoral leadership (a *tragic* cycle), for example, identify a new myth based upon an *empiric* embrace of the demographic change of its surroundings (an *ironic* cycle), which calls for a new style of community-based inquiry into mission, leadership, and even worship? Might the mythical shift allow a church to embrace a new understanding of the gospel in its context, or a synagogue to embrace a new understanding of Torah and its tradition?

Both of these moves toward change, offered by Hopewell's work, are controversial in congregational studies and pastoral leadership literature today. Principal among the objections is the reinterpretation of a congregation's own self-understanding in cultural myths and narratives, especially drawn from literary or cultural studies. However, I would suggest that many of these objections—while difficult for the ethics of research—can be addressed in the ethics of pastoral or rabbinical practice. How might a sermon series take place, for example, that contrasts various myths from local or classical culture (Shakespearean tragedies, perhaps, or even the mythic character of TV wrestling!) to the gospel of Jesus or to rabbinic teachings, to help elevate the congregation's own self-reflection about the narratives it values most? How might an effective narrative pastor or rabbi engage the congregation in retelling its history by identifying key mythical moments of tragic, comic, ironic, or romantic thinking? How might an effective clergy leadership work with a church board to identify conflicting myths among its members, especially related to marker events of great recent importance? Hopewell's mythopoetic approach to congregational imagination elevates the potential for conflict between cultural narratives and those of the gospel/Torah in any congregation. I believe its strength lies in getting to the heart of how many myths or narratives have an unconscious hold on congregational life and the importance of skilled pastoral leadership in helping uncover that mythology with grace and care. Since Hopewell's time, congregational studies has gone on to refine the use of narrative in many of its methods for understanding congregational culture, identity, and mission. In this volume, Larry Peers draws directly on Hopewell.

Early handbooks on congregational studies emphasize this narrative quality of the congregation's story as a foundation for assessing identity and moving into the future. "Story is the way a community usually views, values, and talks about itself in relation to its world and heritage. Most communications in a congregation are narrative in their nature."[1] Through careful observation of church life and local interviews, for example, one can chart the worldview of a church by mapping the most common images and phrases used by members. Numerous phrases like "we prayed for and found a miracle" indicate a romantic worldview; recurring accounts of a departed pastor who was "heroic but embattled" may support a tragic worldview; lots of trust in "everything working out in time" may support a comic worldview; and repeated calls for "facing reality, or fact-finding" may support an ironic worldview. Key phrases and images often provide the portal onto the larger narrative and self-identity of the church.[2]

Some of the most common tools in congregational studies, each of which has a narrative dimension, are the use of *timelines* about a congregation's identity and past, *oral history interviews* that flesh out personal accounts of that history, and the study of *key rituals or celebrations* of a community. Timelines created with leaders or congregational members draw out the corporate memories of key events, leaders, and processes within a temporal sequence, all of which are essential for shaping the congregation's story and resources for change. One study of congregations in transition utilized layered timelines—about the overall history, leadership and key decisions, spiritual and material resources, and buildings—to explore the core values, learnings, and assets from the church's past that might guide them into a new form of ministry in the future.[3] Oral life histories with lifelong or even charter members can flesh out the history in some detail, providing a "long view" memory of congregational assets that might be forgotten in a time of turmoil or abrupt change. Paying special attention to the process and symbolism of defining rituals or celebrations—anniversaries; confirmations; food rituals such as the Fourth of July picnic; or Christmas Eve or Kwanzaa celebrations—helps the observer identify the core images, values, and phrases that mark the congregation's identity or competing identities.[4] Each of these methods draws out "the stories that shape and transmit the memories of a congregation."[5] While congregational studies lie in the background of most of the essays in this volume, Alice Mann draws directly upon this literature.

## Narrative in Practical Theology and Church Practice Literature

Congregational studies has become more nuanced and spiritually focused as it has interfaced with developments in *practical theology*—a field that reflects upon religious practices as they relate to both tradition and local context. This movement from "life to faith and then back to life" is oriented toward regenerating ministry in relation to the congregation's social and cultural context.[6] Whether one identifies this relationship between context and congregation as a "correlation" (Don Browning) or a "dialectic" (Tom Groome), practical theologians generally agree the intersection of community analysis and stories with those of religious tradition and the local congregation can reframe the latter's sense of identity and mission. Educator Kathleen Cahalan writes, "Using narrative in practice provides vivid portraits of people drawn into relationship with God through a wide variety of life situations. . . . Such narratives provide continuity with the past and allow people to see the connection between their lived experience and people from the past: they are connected to the story of salvation history."[7] The intersection of community and congregational stories to revitalize church and synagogue practices has not gone unnoticed in this field, as practical theologian Robert Schreiter writes, "If narratives are the stories that shape our memory, *practices* are the pathways that shape our lives" into the future.[8]

No one in the study of *congregational practices* has done more to link the creative power of narrative work to the revitalization of Christian practices than Diana Butler Bass. Throughout her studies of vital Christian congregations, Bass uncovers the vital links between good narrative work and revitalized practices, both in style and in substance.[9] She writes, "Tradition is embodied in practices. And practices convey meaning through narrative. Without stories, tradition and practice would mean either nothing or anything. And stories—both about the past and the future—are crafted through the imagination."[10]

What Bass has discovered, which much of the religious practices literature has ignored, is the power of well-placed and well-crafted narratives to link congregational practices to both religious tradition and local context. While the relationship between practices, narratives, and tradition is reciprocal and multidirectional, Bass convincingly demonstrates that churches who renew their congregational practices and their tradition almost always place both in a narrative-rich environment where clergy and lay leaders reclaim and retell the old story of their tradition in new ways that intersect with their own lives and time. They exercise a "pastoral imagination" in tandem with their churches' "congregational imagination" in order to reshape these stories of faith.[11] Only by retelling and living their faith stories anew can the dynamic process of "retraditioning" and revitalized practices take place.[12]

The congregations in Bass's research love to tell stories: of individual faith journeys, of their church's past, of their surrounding communities, of their own tradition. However, they do so not just to reclaim the past but primarily to help discern the present and imagine a new future. Several features of this storytelling art emerge:[13]

1. Past stories of decline or struggle are reframed with promise.
2. Church leaders shape stories of meaning by interweaving personal, communal, and biblical accounts.
3. Leaders shape these stories through their own character, but in ways that invite others to place their lives in service to their church and community.
4. The truth of the stories is shown primarily through the authenticity of leaders and the integrity of members as they lived them out.

Each of the "vital congregations" in her research had a full-blown story to tell around one of its key Christian practices, be it hospitality or healing, testimony or discernment, justice or beauty, to name but a few.[14] While many of these practices—and the stories that support them—overlap with those in the literature on Christian practices written by theological educators,[15] ministers and lay leaders gravitate toward Bass's descriptions of ecclesial practices because of the living, congregational contexts from which they are told.

# Systemwide Change:
# Family Systems and Narrative Therapy

~

How does a religious leader bring about lasting change in a faith community or congregation? Two compelling approaches to such change come from the worlds of systems theory and narrative therapy. Each has a narrative dimension—the first implicit, the second explicit. Here, I discuss the work of storying and re-storying the life of a community or organization through these models.

Family systems theory illumines a great deal about how congregations and religious organizations work, especially in the hands of accomplished counselors and consultants like Edwin Friedman and Peter Steinke.[16] The practice of family systems counseling or consulting involves a great deal of storytelling, in part to aid the clients in shaping their own meaning, and in part to inform the consultant about the particular dynamics of the institutional system he or she is working with. While the framework and many images of family systems theory are organic and biological, practitioners of this art are waking up to the power of metaphor and narrative to accomplish what Gregory Bateson, one of the founders of family systems, called a shift in the imagination.[17]

Several key concepts of family systems are illumined by particular kinds of narrative work.[18] *Self-differentiation* of the leader from a congregational system can be deeply enhanced by the *story construction* of a leader's own life and ministry, especially by identifying events and system roles (hero, victim, and so forth) that have created binds similar to ones they face in the present. By learning to narrate their own story and future vision in select ways with others, religious leaders can differentiate their own story from that of the congregation's while still affirming the relationship, especially by inviting members to tell their stories too. Dysfunctional *triangles* in a congregation can be exposed and reshaped by asking each person in the triad to tell his or her version of an event or concern in the presence of others, with an eye toward changes they would like to make. *Systems anxiety*, whether acute or chronic, can be exposed by doing a genealogy of past congregational transitions and conflicts to see how these are repeated now, and by asking newer members of the congregation to share stories and visions largely unaffected by past traumas in the church. A longer view of *homeostasis* in the congregation—especially in times of transition—can be created by telling and retelling the foundational stories of Scripture, founding pastors, and charter families in ways that sustain a viable vision for continuing mission and common life. Overall, family systems theory is enhanced by good narrative work, a point that Susan Beaumont elaborates on in her essay in this volume.

Narrative therapy offers an even more robust vision of how focused story work can transform individuals, families, and organizations, chiefly by reauthoring the operative stories they live by. Developed by Michael White and David Epston, from Australia and New Zealand respectively, this model combines an anthropologist's attention to local stories with a postmodern sensitivity to how knowledge and behavior are socially constructed through narratives.[19] White writes, "Stories provide the framework that makes it possible for us to interpret our experience, and these acts of interpretation are achievements that we take an active part in."[20] Seeking an alternative to classic models of psychotherapy, which rely on a medical model of diagnosis and expert cure, White and Epston develop a social model of retrieving, deconstructing, and reshaping the basic narratives that fund the meaning and practices of everyday life.

Narrative therapy arises from a postmodern worldview based largely on the work of the French social theorist Michel Foucault. This framework has several strengths. First, the narratives we live by, handed down by culture and religious tradition, are so internalized that we may not see an alternative to them, especially when they become dysfunctional or unable to adapt to changing conditions. Second, these internalized narratives can be deconstructed by naming the ways they dominate or control our own lives. Finally, received narratives can be reconstructed or replaced by re-storying our lives according to newfound strengths and capacities for change. In other words, narrative therapists use this postmodern worldview to map the ways that dominant, often outworn narratives can be externalized, then reconstructed to direct our social practices and discourse in fundamentally new directions. Basic to this whole framework is the assumption that each of us, and each community or organization we work with, is a coauthor in shaping the narratives that provide frameworks of meaning and practice for our lives.

In this volume, articles by Larry Peers and Susan Nienaber describe in more detail how narrative therapy actually works.[21] By narrating one's experiences, externalizing the problem-saturated story, identifying "sparkling" moments that allow one to step out of that story, and by historicizing these unique moments into a new story, these consultants and the congregations they work with begin to re-story their lives for a more promising future. However, this is no easy task. Most congregations have multiple stories of what happened in the past— particularly in times of transition or controversy. Helping all parties give voice to their versions of the story is a necessary step to beginning the work of externalizing the problem. Only then can the problem be separated from personalities, and the natural mechanism of scapegoating be replaced with forming a new alliance against the problem. For example, I knew a historic urban congregation that came to see its struggle to find "the right pastor" as a series of mismatched personalities, each of which was summarily dismissed. Only over time did the church come to see the abiding problem it had created was misplaced expectations for a pulpiteer, community organizer, and even national figure based on a period of its life that had long since passed. By jettisoning this beloved but now dysfunctional image of the right pastor, the congregation was able to forge a new image of spiritual director and community builder that fit its current age of life.

Because narrative work for change in a congregation is so collaborative and communal, it presents numerous challenges. How does the narrative leader help a community sift through the multiple stories of the past to build consensus around the presenting problem and how it has dominated their lives? How can the leader and community link the various shining moments of stepping out of that story into a history of alternative experiences and assets that form the basis of a new story? How does the leader help relate the ongoing changes and transience of congregational and community stories with the stories of the faith that have more staying power and authority—like Scripture and religious tradition? Is this congregation free to change any or all of these stories, or does story reconstruction vary at these different levels? The complexity and collaborative nature of this work means that narrative change will take time, multiple voices, and a leader who remains focused on the reconstructive narrative work at hand. Helping a community of faith re-vision its personal and collective narratives is one of the greatest leadership challenges of the age.[22]

## Adaptive Leadership
## and Organizational Storytelling

~

*Adaptive leadership* is a kind of leading, championed by Ron Heifetz, Sharon Parks, and others at Harvard, that focuses on the values-oriented leader who helps an organization distinguish between what is essential and nonessential in a period of rapid change.[23] This adaptive work is distinguished from the more technical sides of management and problem solving because it helps the organization close the gap between long-held values and changing realities. The most important leadership in an organization, then, is not the day-to-day management of problems according to expertise but the risk-taking *adaptive leaders* who help everyone in the organization rethink their practice and reshape it in line with a new, adaptive vision. While changing realities can be managed, they rarely can be changed altogether. Instead, it is our values and behaviors that need to change. Adaptive leadership requires steady personal presence, being attuned to the learning needs and assets of a community, and drawing on that community to develop new strategies of encountering problems, primarily through collaborative learning.

By building on Heifetz's understanding of adaptive work as closing the gap between values and reality, Sharon Parks describes in detail how this work involves the use of personal presence, image, and metaphor, all of which are integral to good storytelling. In her thoughtful work, *Leadership Can Be Taught: A Bold Approach for a Complex World*, Parks describes how Heifetz teaches students at the Harvard Kennedy School, and she interviews students about the lasting impact of their leadership course with him.[24] One of Heifetz's strengths is to use the classroom as a laboratory for developing personal presence, which is a palpable quality of connecting, staying with, and improvising in relation to one's audience. He uses classroom reading—usually of poetry or inspirational literature chosen by the students—and coaches them in how to persuade others of its power and truth. Then he asks students to create a song on the spot, focusing only on the "music beneath the words," by humming or creating syllabic tunes that convey his or her feel for the piece. This improvisational and oral art is a key to freeing up presence and helping students learn the value of timing, intonation, gesture, and silence.

When Parks interviews students, she finds that many of these on-the-spot encounters in the classroom stay with them, and they attach to them various images and metaphors from the course. In other words, key phrases and metaphors become tools of action and leadership performance. Some of the more lasting phrases are publicly accessible, even to outsiders: "work avoidance activity," "listening for the 'hidden issue,'" and "giving the work back to the group." Most of the interviewees picked up these phrases as action guides to describe their own newly acquired practice of leadership in their work settings. Other metaphors are thicker and must be unpacked to outsiders, like "going to the dance floor, then to the balcony" to capture the activities of intervening or joining with colleagues in an action, and then observing from a vantage point to see how they respond; or "using yourself as a barometer" to describe using self-awareness in the moment—like one's anxiety or fear—as a teaching moment to connect with others (who probably are feeling the same thing). One of the key images of the course, "doing the pizza," actually visualizes a relational and power analysis of a key work activity. By placing the X as the core work at the center, one then diagrams the circles of involved parties and stakeholders (the pepperoni), how they are clumped into group or departmental interests (the slices), and then ways that different groups in different slices are communicating about the problems with others.

While Heifetz stresses the use of personal presence and embodiment, the intuitive assessment of shared experience through key phrases or metaphors, and the modeling of creative deviance, steadiness, and imagination in the person of the leader, Parks lifts out aspects of adaptive leadership that become communal practices and are closely related to narrative work. As leaders employ key metaphors and images from the course, they are taking on a specific role in a community drama, which soon unfolds as a narrative of leader interaction and community response. Some phrases and metaphors identify spaces for engaging in certain kinds of activity, like the intervention of the "dance floor" or the careful observation of the "balcony." Others are invitations to draw others into shared work, like "turning the work over to the group," in ways that can be narrated as collaborative action. Finally, "doing the pizza" captures in a single image a complex, narrative analysis of the social networks and power relations involved in a core activity. Much of what Heifetz and Parks advocate for leadership formation, then, involves the basic foundations of good story work. The essays in this book by Gil Rendle and Larry Peers draw on this literature.

Others in leadership theory have developed storytelling into one of the basic arts of organizational leadership. One of the gurus in this development is Stephen Denning, who draws upon his own experience of using development stories from the field to help transform the World Bank into a leader not only in lending but also in information management. In a helpful book *The Leader's Guide to Storytelling: Mastering the Art and Discipline of Business*, Denning identifies the elements, patterns, and strategies of storytelling that can elicit organization-wide change, even in complex institutions.[25] Change-oriented storytelling has four key elements: a *style* that is personal, simple and clear, and authentic; a fearless presentation of *the truth* that everyone can grasp and with no hedging or mixed messages; a balance of *preparation*, knowing the shape and details of the story, with spontaneity in telling it; and a total immersion of yourself in the story *delivery* by being fully present to the audience, an impromptu reliving of the story, and lively use of gesture, intonation, and imagery. Through it all, effective storytelling must be well placed, when an audience is awake and ready, and perfectly timed, usually in seconds not minutes, to evoke a new insight or shift in the imagination.

Denning also focuses on what he calls a "storytelling catalog" that outlines the various kinds of stories leaders can use and how they function. Here is a brief summary of what various kinds of stories can do:

Spark action: springboard stories that dramatize how a person or a group develops new resources or capacities to change a crucial situation—with a happy outcome

Communicate who you are: stories that build trust in you as a leader, with rich enough detail and personal disclosure to convey the gist of your character

Communicate who the organization is: stories that relay the promise of a community or an organization, what it can deliver, and how it has done so

Transmit values: stories that lay out the norms for how a community operates—what is constructive behavior and what is not, as in "We don't do those kind of things around here; instead we try to . . ."

Foster collaboration: one person's account of what this community means to him or her, and using it to elicit other stories across the room and embody the kind of collaboration and trust hoped for in the organization

Tame the grapevine: the informal network of communication and coffee-pot gossip, and tapping it to sideline false rumors with more accurate stories or even humorous anecdotes about what would really happen if that were true

Share knowledge: stories about what a group has learned this week, what project it is discovering, told regularly in order to help various teams or departments in the organization share knowledge

Prepare for the future: stories that open people's imaginations to what lies ahead—challenges and possibilities—and that affirm the organization's ability to face those challenges

Many of these story types and functions are part of the work of the consultants whose essays appear in this volume. The trick for leaders is to know what type to employ when, and to have a ready-made repertoire of various kinds of stories for different situations and challenges.

One of Denning's colleagues in the business narrative business, John Seely Brown, explores the power of cultivating community-wide narrative practices, in addition to the leader's use of storytelling.[26] He focuses on the power of social meaning-making through stories and how narratives have the unique ability to tap the "tacit knowledge" that is part of much organizational behavior and practice. In other words, most communities and organizations have inherited ways of doing things that embody much of their implicit knowledge in social practices— like welcoming newcomers, celebrating achievements and anniversaries, or reflecting upon failures. This native wisdom can be made more explicit through storytelling around some of these best practices. And when inherited practices become onerous or no longer are constructive, good storytelling can honor what they accomplished in the past, cull the wisdom that was there, and help reframe new practices for the future. Community-wide storytelling, in this way, helps make tacit knowing explicit and open to reframing. It also helps the organization share its common, often closeted wisdom more effectively with the entire community and with newcomers. Storytelling is a powerful tool in information sharing, especially at the level of common practice.

## Narrative and Change

In this chapter I have focused on the multiple arenas of knowledge production and leadership practice where good narrative work takes place and has been documented. Some of these arenas, like congregational studies and organizational storytelling, are more developed in their narrative reflection and theorizing, while others, like adaptive leadership, are just beginning to make the connections. By sharing these various frameworks and strategies of narrative work that can bring about change, I hope to provide a richer background for appreciating the consultant essays that follow. And I hope that congregational and other religious leaders realize that many of their colleagues, including members of their own organizations, already know a great deal about good narrative practice and can become excellent collaborators in bringing about change in their houses or communities of faith.

## NOTES

1. Jackson Carroll, Carl Dudley, and William McKinney, eds., *Handbook for Congregational Studies* (Nashville: Abingdon, 1986).

2. Nancy Ammerman, Jackson Carroll, Carl Dudley, and William McKinney, *Studying Congregations: A New Handbook* (Nashville: Abingdon, 1998), 96–97.

3. Carl Dudley and Nancy Ammerman, *Congregations in Transition: A Guide for Analyzing, Assessing, and Adapting in Changing Communities* (San Francisco: Jossey-Bass, 2002), chap. 3.

4. Ammerman et al, *Studying Congregations*, chap. 3.

5. Ibid., 33.

6. Ibid., 25.

7. Kathleen Cahalan, "Introducing Ministry and Fostering Integration: Teaching the Bookends of the Master of Divinity Program," in *For Life Abundant: Practical Theology, Theological Education, and Christian Ministry*, eds., Dorothy C. Bass and Craig Dykstra (Grand Rapids: Eerdmans, 2008), 108.

8. Robert Schreiter, quoted in Cahalan, "Introducing Ministry and Fostering Integration," 34.

9. This theme runs through Diana Butler Bass's research of local congregations: *The Practicing Congregation: Imagining a New Old Church* (Herndon, VA: Alban Institute, 2004); *From Nomads to Pil-*

*grims: Stories from Practicing Congregations* (Herndon, VA: Alban Institute, 2006), and *Christianity for the Rest of Us: How the Neighborhood Church Is Transforming the Faith* (San Francisco: HarperSanFrancisco, 2006).

10. Diana Butler Bass, *Practicing Congregation*, 95.

11. Ibid., 94.

12. Ibid., 42.

13. My interpretation of Diana Butler Bass's four features of narrative leadership in "Living the Story," foreword to *Leadership in Congregations*, ed. Richard Bass (Herndon, VA: Alban Institute, 2006), ix–xv.

14. These are outlined most clearly in Diana Butler Bass, *Christianity for the Rest of Us*, although leaders from many of these churches wrote their congregation's story in Diana Butler Bass, *From Nomads to Pilgrims*.

15. See Dorothy Bass, ed., *Practicing Our Faith: A Way of Life for Searching People* (San Francisco: Jossey-Bass, 1997), and Miroslav Volf and Dorothy Bass, eds., *Practicing Theology* (Grand Rapids: Eerdmans, 2002).

16. Edwin H. Friedman, *Generation to Generation: Family Process in Church and Synagogue* (New York: Guilford Press, 1985), esp. sec. 3; and Peter Steinke, *How Your Church Family Works: Understanding Congregations as Emotional Systems* (Herndon, VA: Alban Institute, 2006).

17. Authors who expand family systems theory to narrative practices include Paul C. Rosenblatt, *Metaphors of Family Systems Theory: Toward New Constructions* (New York: Guilford Press, 1997); and Renos K. Papadopoulos and John Byng-Hall, eds., *Multiple Voices: Narrative in Systemic Family Psychotherapy*, Tavistock Clinic Series (New York: Routledge, 1998).

18. See, for example, Ronald W. Richardson, *Becoming a Healthier Pastor: Family Systems Theory and the Pastor's Own Family* (Minneapolis: Fortress Press, 2004).

19. Michael White and David Epston, *Narrative Means to Therapeutic Ends* (New York: W. W. Norton, 1990).

20. Michael White, "The Narrative Perspective in Therapy," in *Re-authoring Lives: Interviews and Essays* (Adelaide, South Australia: Dulwich Center Publications, 1995).

21. See also Gerald Monk, John Winslade, Kathie Crocket, David Epston, eds., *Narrative Therapy in Practice: The Archaeology of Hope* (San Francisco: Jossey-Bass, 1996), and Michael White, *Maps of Narrative Practice* (New York: W. W. Norton, 2007).

22. Alan Parry and Robert E. Doan, *Story Re-Visions: Narrative Therapy in the Postmodern World* (New York: Guilford Press, 1994).

23. Ronald A. Heifetz, *Leadership Without Easy Answers* (Cambridge, MA: Belknap Press, 1994).

24. Sharon Daloz Parks, *Leadership Can Be Taught: A Bold Approach for a Complex World* (Cambridge: Harvard Business School Press, 2005).

25. Stephen Denning, *The Leader's Guide to Storytelling: Mastering the Art and Discipline of Business Narrative* (San Francisco: Jossey-Bass, 2005).

26. John Seely Brown, Stephen Denning, Katalina Groh, and Laurence Prusak, *Storytelling in Organizations: Why Storytelling Is Transforming 21st Century Organizations and Management* (Burlington, MA: Butterworth-Heinemann, 2005).

# CHAPTER 2

# Narrative Leadership and Renewed Congregational Identity

~

## GIL RENDLE

Leaders seem to know or strongly intuit that stories are powerful and can be used either to shape or to block ministry. Depending upon the story, who uses the story, and how it is used, a well-placed story can transform a ministry situation. Powerful stories work. Try to offer proof, and others will respond with alternative theories and explanations. Offer facts and figures, and the response is often a debate of the data or its interpretation. But tell a good story, a bold story, and people will connect deeply and respond without explanation. A good story invites and draws forward a response. It is like telling a joke in a group of joke tellers. Hearing one joke, someone in the group inevitably responds, "Have you heard the one about . . . ," which prompts another—and then another. Soon the group is living in a sea of smiles and laughter that could not be prompted by explaining how irony works or the way humor derails assumptions with a new twist or surprise.

We know stories work and they are powerful. But how? And why? And why now? If clergy have for so long used stories to carry the freight for their preaching, why is the conversation now turning to the use of stories as a transaction of leadership? Suddenly the connection of stories to leadership—narrative leadership—seems to be a long-held assumption newly discovered. If you do an Internet search for "narrative leadership," the result will be a plethora of references mixed throughout the various disciplines of law, medicine, therapy, nursing, politics, art, theology, . . . and the list goes on. If we have known about the power of stories for so long, why has attention to this part of leadership heated up now? This essay offers a brief answer to why stories have become newly important and an introduction to the role of leaders in shaping and using stories as part of the exercise of leadership.

In a book of essays about narrative leadership, it is reasonable to begin with a good story. This particular story is a story of a congregation told by its pastor. The setting is a small urban congregation in a changed and changing neighborhood. In many places across the nation, similar congregations might tell a story of struggle and depletion. But this time the story is a tale of risk, humor, and new discoveries for the pastor and the people.

## A STORY OF BROADWAY CHURCH

### Written and told by Mike Mather, pastor

During Advent and Lent we have weekly evening prayers at Broadway. A few years ago during Advent a strange thing happened. It had been snowing that Wednesday evening, so when we gathered for evening prayers, only six of us were there. As we got near the time when we would be praying together, there were loud sounds of teenagers at the side door of the church. As people were reflecting on the Scripture reading in silence, I got up and moved to the door. A young man no older than thirteen who was standing at the door asked me what was going on. I told him we were having evening prayers. He asked if he and his two friends could come in. I considered that for a moment—I wasn't sure it would be a good idea. But of course I said, "Sure."

The young man and his buddies came in and sat down. We continued in silence for another few seconds and then moved into the hymn "Standing in the Need of Prayer." I heard the side door of the church open again, and more young voices. As the gathered body sang, I moved back to the door. There were three more young men. "Are our friends here?" they asked. "Yes," I answered. "Would you get 'em and tell 'em to come out?" they asked. I considered it, but then said, "No. But you're welcome to join them if you wish." Honestly, I was hoping a little bit that they would say no. But they didn't. They followed me into the sanctuary. They came and knelt down next to the first young man who had spoken to me, and they whispered hurriedly. Clearly, they were asking him to leave. But he shook his head, and the others sat down, not particularly any happier than I was.

I explained how our prayer time worked: Anyone could offer a prayer; and when a person finished offering a prayer, he or she would say, "Lord, in your mercy," and everyone else would say, "Hear our prayer." The prayer time began. I invited prayers for people in the congregation. There was silence and I heard the young people start to chatter. I was almost at the point of saying something when one of the Broadway members offered a prayer and closed with "Lord, in your mercy," and everyone said, "Hear our prayer." I must confess that my eyes were open and on the young people. When they heard everyone say, "Hear our prayer," I noticed that their open eyes got very wide. They started to offer prayers. "For my cousin Booder, who was killed last year," one of the young people said. He rushed to the words, "Lord, in your mercy," and everyone said, "Hear our prayer."

Now all the young people were offering prayers for people in their families—many of them people who had been killed. The teenagers were all noticeably eager to hear everyone joining them with "Hear our prayer." We prayed for the world, and people offered prayers for places of violence around the world. We prayed for our community; one of the young people prayed "that the schools would stop expellin' people" and everyone said, "Hear our prayer." The time of prayer reached a height, though, when the young man who was the leader said, "For me and for my grandma, 'cuz my dad is tryin' to take me away from her." And everyone said, "Hear our prayer."

I invited people to turn in their hymnal to where the Lord's Prayer is printed, and we prayed it together. Then we sang "I Want to Walk as a Child of the Light." Those young people stayed and exchanged signs of peace along with everyone else. And then they left—much quieter than they had come."[1]

The story itself is a good story, well written and well told by a creative United Methodist pastor. The story, however, is not leadership in itself. Rather it is the opportunity and the potential tool for leadership. This becomes quite apparent as Mike tells the rest of the story, which came to belong to the congregation in part as a consequence of what Mike did with the story. He writes, "A year and half later, when we had all noticed that our ministry with young people had expanded dramatically, we received a grant from the national church to expand and build on our work with young people. At least in my mind, we were able to trace it back to our openness in worship that snowy evening in Advent."[2]

## How Do Stories Work?

Mike's story of his church is powerful to read. This is in part because he is a good story writer and a great storyteller. The story advances in stages. His own qualms about the situation provide some humor and connection with the reader and hearer. The telling moves us into deep human feelings. Finally, the end leaves no doubt that something has changed in both the lives of the young boys and the few church members who were there. However, to get from that Advent evening experience to a denominational grant that supports ministry with young people, Mike had to tell this story to congregational leaders, congregational members, the wider community, and the United Methodist denomination in a way that would allow and encourage people to see not only what did happen but also what could happen.

How stories become such tools of leadership can be a rather detailed and theoretical discussion of a range of issues, such as earned versus attributed authority of the storyteller, the physiology of the brain and how narrative information is processed, or the role of dominant cultural motifs in carrying meaning. In this brief essay, however, I want to focus on the difference between logic and intuition.

Explanation (persuasive leadership) engages logic. Explanation gives people *reasons* based on proof supported by facts, figures, and theory. Stories (narrative leadership) engage *intuition*. My favored definition of intuition is "practiced wisdom." Stories engage people deeply because they tell people what is already known, or already hoped for, but not readily apparent because the truth, or the possibility of the truth, has not surfaced to conscious awareness. People *know* from life experience. But what is known lies beneath their awareness until uncovered, at which point the knowledge becomes obvious. To uncover the truth and acknowledge a possibility requires risk taking or courage. Give people facts (persuasive leadership engaging reason), and the conversation stumbles over agreement or disputation of the facts. Give people a good story, a bold story, and the conversation intuitively leaps ahead to action, allowing people to *know* and to give meaning to the action.

This intuitive leap to understanding and action is what Stephen Denning, program director of knowledge management at the World Bank, calls "the springboard effect." Denning writes about springboard stories, by which he means "a story that enables a leap in understanding by the audience so as to grasp how an organization or community or complex system may change."[3] He writes from his own experience as the newly appointed information officer at the World Bank in 1996. His task was to help the World Bank, which was understood to be a *financial* institution, come to terms with the shift to an *information*-based economy. The real power of the World Bank lay in the embedded information and knowledge it had, which could be more effective in advancing development in underdeveloped countries than the billions of dollars in loans it made each year.

However, the identity of the World Bank as a *bank* was so longstanding that even astute leaders were deaf to explorations of the potential power the World Bank held if it could develop effective ways to share information and network people around this knowledge. Despite the new potential, Denning's presentations got little response. People were not connecting to what Denning offered. Remember that the year was 1996 and the potential availability and use of information on the Web had yet to be discovered.

In the midst of Denning's frustrations, a colleague shared a simple story over lunch about a recent trip to Zambia, which at that time had one of the poorest infrastructures of any nation. About the size of France with only one-fifth the population, income and resources were so scarce that health care was close to nonexistent. The story told by his colleague was of a health worker in Kamana, a small town about six hundred kilometers from Lusaka, the capital of Zambia.[4] The health worker was looking for a solution to a problem in treating malaria. The health worker logged onto the Centers for Disease Control and Prevention website in Atlanta and got the answer to his problem. The knowledge was readily available in the health systems of the United States but did not exist in the health care system in Zambia. The information quickly saved lives in Zambia without making additional demands on the available resources.

A simple story—almost too simple in our own present-day experience of the unending resources accessible through the Internet. In fact, Denning himself did not recognize the story's power except as a simple anecdote of the kind of change he was arguing for in the World Bank. However, to Denning's surprise, it was this simple story that captured people's attention. Despite all of the explanations using theory, facts, figures, and graphs he had on hand for his presentations, only when Denning told the story of the health worker did the lights go on and people began to respond with, "Of course!" The people listening to Denning's presentations now seemed to leap past his explanations to intuitions and discussions about their own experience in the World Bank.

### JEWISH TEACHING STORY

Truth, naked and cold, had been turned away from every door in the village. Her nakedness frightened the people. When Parable found her she was huddled in a corner, shivering and hungry. Taking pity on her, Parable gathered her up and took her home. There she dressed Truth in story, warmed her, and sent her out again. Clothed in story, Truth knocked again at the villagers' doors and was readily welcomed into the people's houses. They invited her to eat at their table and warm herself by their fire.[5]

Mike Mather's story of young people slipping into a snowy Advent prayer service is a simple story, a good story. Like Denning's simple story of a health care worker in Zambia, Mike's story becomes narrative leadership at the point that Mike tells it in a way that helps people see past what happened and grasp the implications for what could happen. It becomes a parable of possibility, like the Jewish story above.

Statistics might have helped. Statistics about the youth in the community and the rise of crime are terribly important for the leaders of the congregation to know. But this was a small urban church of older adults who remember when the community was safer and when their congregation was stronger; statistics alone would produce only worry and fear about the plight of the congregation in a changing neighborhood.

The mandate of the gospel to reach out to the least, the lost, and the lonely is important for any Christian congregation in a changing community to rehearse through Bible study, prayer, and discussion. But the people in such congregations often see the huge needs and risks around them and think only of the limits and timidity of their own resources. Studies and discussions of the changing community often remain studies and discussions.

In the hands of a narrative leader, however, a story moves people beyond fears toward hope, beyond remembered pasts to present and future potential, beyond limited resources to unbounded possibility. When Mike tells this story to the people of Broadway church, new messages not available in statistics and Bible study discussions emerge; messages such as:

+ You can do this.
+ You know how to talk to young people.
+ These young people are willing and eager to talk with you.
+ You have something they need.
+ When you offer yourselves, they will receive.
+ This ministry with youth is you.

## Safe and Weak Stories

Congregations, particularly mainline and established congregations, commonly tell either safe or weak stories about themselves. In part, this is an inheritance of mainline and established congregations' disestablishment in the changing democratic culture. In an earlier era, when identity and purpose were clearer for many congregations, stories could be bold and have the strength of pride: "We are *the* Methodist church in town." "Our Unitarian church was founded by descendents of original Pilgrim families and has always been located here on the town green."

However, cultural preferences and demographic changes have shifted away from many mainline and established congregations, especially those that have long lived in areas that people are moving away from (or in areas where the population has changed). Like a once-strong mother church that experiences schism from a "daughter" faction, what is left behind are questions and uncertainty. The daughter faction often positions itself against what was once assumed, which provides a strong story—and sense of identity—for the new daughter to live out. The mother church is left with a much weaker story that wonders why those who were once friends and family would choose against their established relationship.

Today many clergy are still called or appointed to—and many lay leaders inherit—congregations with *weak* stories that are products of a remembered past that had position and resources. Some leaders still wrestle with the memory of the sanctuary filled every Sunday, while they now measure the increasing distance between fewer worshipers who scatter themselves across the pews in the same sanctuary. Many congregations tell their stories using measurements of how many people used to attend, how many programs they once had, how they once did mission using the resources from an oversubscribed budget. They also "remember" how their clergy once knew everyone in the church, were well known in the community, and never preached a bad sermon.

Telling a weak congregational story does not depend upon having a shrinking membership or inheriting a changing neighborhood. A strong, vital, and large congregation today can still tell a weak story. With hundreds in attendance, multiple programs, and growing staff, it is nonetheless possible to live out of weakness as a story is told of community needs too large for the church to address, community issues too complex to lend themselves to change, and ... there is always a larger church up the street better equipped.

If many congregations have learned to tell weak stories, many more tell *safe* stories. Safe stories are the ones people tell themselves that are true but incomplete. A safe story is about how warm and friendly the congregation is. What is incomplete is the rest of the story about how stiff and formal members are with visitors while being warm and friendly with the folk who attend regularly. What is safe is the story of how the congregation was once a neighborhood church that had the gift of including people from each new immigrant wave that washed into its neighborhood. What is incomplete is how members now feel distant and distrustful of the new people surrounding the church who seem so different from them. We collude not to tell the rest of the story that will make us uncomfortable.

Safe stories may be even more difficult for a congregation to live past than weak stories, because safe stories are self-shaped and self-imposed. Novelist and philosopher Iris Murdoch suggests that people commonly live out of a distorted perception of themselves, which might be thought of as a "safe middle."[6] She suggests that we present our safe middle to ourselves because it is a true though incomplete reflection and it is comfortable for us to live with. What is missing from the safe-middle identity on one side is the darker side of our limitations, our problems, and our challenges, which feel too risky for us to acknowledge publicly. If we included our darker side in our descriptions of ourselves, we would actually have to do something about them. What is also missing from the safe-middle identity on the other side is the stronger side that includes our gifts and our talents. If we name our gifts and talents, we would actually have to use them and be accountable for them.

So it is that I, from the protected middle, introduce myself to others—and think about myself—in safe ways, where I experience less challenge and more comfort and where I hide the limitations that I face and the gifts and strengths I have developed. So too, congregations tend to live out of a similar safe middle where limiting issues are not acknowledged openly and gifts are both unnamed and underused so that risk is never confronted.

## "You're Better than That!"

A central task of the narrative leader is to learn deeply about the people and the history of the congregation and, when they are found to be limited by weakness and are retreating to safety, to be able to tell the people stories that carry the message, "You're better than that." Howard Gardner, author and Harvard professor of education, in his writing about leadership describes a central task of leadership as giving the people a better story to live.[7]

Giving people a better story to live by is not an invention of a new tale to tell about themselves, not a Pollyannaish telling of what isn't. In fact, telling a better story is an act of leadership because it tells a true story of the people that is different from the safe way in which they choose to tell their own story. Such telling, for the leader, is risky. This kind of storied leadership challenges the weak or the safe story that has been chosen in the past simply because it has been so comfortable and undemanding. Narrative leadership risks telling a new and different story that will disrupt established harmonies and entail costs even though it is an effort at faithfulness. Whenever leadership takes risks, there are possible consequences.

## Leading People to Their New Story

In his book on dialogue, William Isaacs, a long-term participant in the dialogue project begun by David Bohm, provides a dialogue map that moves groups through four stages:[8]

+ politeness
+ breakdown
+ inquiry
+ flow

A dialogue map can be thought of as the path the leader follows to get to the better story. The four stages move groups not only to mature and sustaining dialogue but also to authentic community and missional purpose because, at the end, a new identity is unveiled.

A similar four-stage process of group development, through which the identity and purpose of group relationships (as well as friendships, marriages, and other associations) move toward maturity, is recognized in the disciplines of organizational development and management:[9]

+ forming
+ storming
+ norming
+ performing

The path leads from group inception to maturity, which, when well managed, allows for both deep relationships and productiveness.

Using these two developmental constructs in tandem, I will describe the movements of effective narrative leadership.

## Stage 1: Politeness and Forming

In the development of relationships, politeness and forming characterize the initial stage of getting to know another person. In marriage, it is courtship. Politeness and forming are the heart of the common advice to pastors to not change anything for a year until they know the people and the congregation. Developmentally, the group question being addressed in this earliest stage of community is, "Do we belong together?" What is being tested is whether the "you" and the "I" have enough similarities to allow us to remain together. Will we understand and appreciate one another? Can I trust you with me? Can you appreciate me without needing me to change?

For this first stage to be a time of politeness is natural. As in most courtships, it begins with putting one's best foot forward. I will tell you stories about myself that will invite empathy, understanding, and appreciation. For many congregations, this is clearly the place where weak and safe stories of themselves live: "All of our children grew up and moved away, and there are no children in our Sunday school any more." "We don't have to add any ministries because there are so many young couples and families moving into our area that we have eight to ten new visitors every Sunday." "We used to be able to have large groups of adult classes, but we were younger back then." "We've always been great at caring for anyone in the congregation who had a need." "We've never tithed here because most of our people are on limited incomes, but if there is a problem like the parking lot or the boiler all you need to do is ask and we'll have what we need by the next Sunday."

The dialogue at this stage of the relationship is, in fact, shared monologues. People tell their stories to one another with only the expectation that they will be listened to without being challenged or changed. The question at this stage is whether people will accept and appreciate one another under the conditions described by these stories that so often focus on weakness or safety. "That's just the way it is." We have no expectation that our stories will actually engage one another, and it would be impolite to suggest that our stories could be different.

This is the familiar honeymoon phase for new clergy or leaders entering the congregation. Clergy and leaders will often seek to extend this comfortable stage of harmony for lengthened periods by "don't ask, don't tell" practices, even though they inhibit growth toward more faithful ministry.

## Stage 2: Breakdown and Storming

Breakdown and storming characterize the stage at which narrative leadership—as distinct from storytelling—first kicks in. In the dynamics of group development, the central question shifts from "Do we belong together?" to "Who's in control?" Is there only one way for the congregation to tell its story here, or will people allow their leaders to tell it in a way that might be riskier and less comfortable?

Many small urban congregations currently tell their stories in safe, weak ways about how the congregation used to have more people who gave more money and had more children; but now they are older, the neighborhood is changed, crime has increased, and neighborhood youth are scary. The act of narrative leadership at this second stage is for the leader to offer the telling of a different story, a better story, for the people to live. For Mike to tell his people their own tale of a snowy Advent prayer service and then remind them that they don't need to be afraid is an act of storied leadership. Instead, the new story tells them, "You can do this."

Such a new life story for the congregation is neither Pollyannaish nor fabricated. There exists a real springboard of experience from which to tell the new story. And because Mike reminds them of the thrill and the power that they themselves felt at the end of that snowy evening, new resources of the Spirit are unleashed and can be used to claim grant money and engage the community and its youth in new ways.

Do not miss the fact that this second stage is marked by breakdown and storming. To introduce new, bolder, better stories of ministry and faithfulness for the future is destabilizing to the congregation that has learned its story in another form. Such new stories challenge old identities and comforts in which people knew how to *be*. Such new stories challenge *familiar relationships* with unknown and *untested purposes*. And most congregations are fundamentally more relational than purposeful.[10]

The leader's introduction of a new story in this second stage must be marked by *controlled* discussion and *skillful* conversation. It requires the "holding environment" of leadership theorist Ronald Heifetz's adaptive leadership.[11] Introducing a new story does not begin with *evaluative* statements of what is wrong with remembering the past in a certain way or what is wrong when people feel captive to current changes. It does depend upon the *descriptive* telling of stories of what could be, based on the real experience of the people in the current moment. Evaluation invites resistance; description invites conversation.

In this second stage, for the first time the conversation is about identity, about who the congregation is; it is an actual dialogue more than it is shared monologues. The dialogue depends upon engagement.

## Stage 3: Inquiry and Norming

At the third stage of the development of the relationship and the story of the congregation, the "new" is created. In terms of group life, the initial questions, "Do we belong together?" and "Who is in charge?" have now moved on to the third question of "Okay, now that we see things differently, how will we move ahead?" This is the norming stage, because new agreements, or norms, about what is important and how the congregation will behave are being established, based on what was learned in the first two stages.

From a narrative perspective, this is the stage of inquiry because it is *shared* dialogue in which leader and people together look for a new way to tell their story. In truth, good leaders do not show up with the new story (*the* vision, *the* answer) in hand, ready to be delivered for others to implement. Such stories, visions, answers are notoriously resisted when imposed by leaders because they are not authentic to the people's experience and do not arise from the interchange between God, the people, and the leader.

The stage of norming and inquiry is a messy time of creating the new story based on a complex dialogue that can never really be directed or controlled. It is dialogue between multiple partners: the leader; the people; God's will for the people; the

teachings of holy text and of tradition, history, and context. The
new story can only be discovered in reflective dialogue among
all these voices. This is the central discovery of Nobel-winning
physicist and world-acclaimed thinker David Bohm: that the
new always comes from the speaking and the listening involved
in dialogue.[12] When I say something while you listen, and then
you respond, often I realize that your response means that you
heard something more than I thought I had said. You learned
from what I said, and in turn, I learned from the new thing
that I heard in your response. Such sustained dialogues, which
depend as much on listening as on speaking, lead over time to
new insights and actions that neither person could have discovered or dreamed up on his or her own.

In the inquiry and norming stage, the temporal frame of
reference changes. In the first two stages, time is linear; it is
*chronos*; it can be planned and controlled. In the forming stage,
clergy routinely use their first months of entry into a congregation to intentionally learn stories. In the storming stage, congregations routinely and safely use periodic practices of visioning,
strategic planning, or discernment to engage the assumptions
of current stories with controlled and skillful discussions of
exploration. In the third stage of inquiry and norming, the dynamics of time shift from *chronos* to *kairos*, as time now is God's
and requires operating beyond a set timetable. At this stage the
norming and inquiry take as long as they take, until a shift to
a new story is made. The leader's task is to keep people safely
involved and engaged in dialogue that allows discovery about
themselves and their ministry.

## Stage 4: Flow and Performing

This final stage of flow and performing is the arena of maturity
where a new authenticity of dialogue and community is lived
out. Finding the right story, the bold and faithful story, can

provide life and purpose for a congregation over an extended period.

Quite a few years ago, Bob Pierson became the pastor of Christ United Methodist Church, an urban congregation in Tulsa, struggling with the changing environment around it. Worship attendance had shrunk to less than two hundred people by the time he arrived. Other churches around Christ United were either dying or relocating. As pastor and leader, Bob carefully invited and structured a new conversation with the congregation in which its current story was challenged. Participants in the conversation intentionally asked what Jesus would do in their situation, and this conversation prompted a risk to reach out to the people who lived in the neighborhood around Christ United who had needs, particularly people who were divorced. Members of the congregation began to retell their story as "the Good Samaritan Church."[13] Using the familiar biblical story, they noted that the good Samaritan did a number of things: he paid attention and didn't turn a blind eye to the pain around him; he went out of his way to see the one who was hurt; he got involved; he made a difference; and he stayed in relationship while the person healed. In the years that followed, the congregation entered a time of learning how to live out its new story—how to pay attention, how to see what others would rather not, how to get involved, and how to develop lasting relationships. Christ Church's future required much learning and risking. But it was sustained by its new story of being the Good Samaritan Church, which provided what is described in this fourth stage as "flow." Flow is the natural living out of an authentic story and carries the people well beyond any future that the leader or the people could have anticipated. When Bob retired as senior pastor, the church—still located in the same declining neighborhood, in an older facility, and with limited parking—had an average worship attendance of seventeen hundred people. While not all new and authentic stories lead to massive numerical growth, they can hold massive energy and provide faithful purpose.

## Living Out Identity

Narrative leadership is relational, interactive, and long term. In his article describing what a college president (really) does, J. Gordon Kingsley, then president of William Jewell College in Liberty, Missouri, suggested the real work behind all the public activity that people see in the president's role is the need "to learn the song of the tribe in order to sing the song of the tribe so that others can find their place in the song and then together write the next verse."[14] To reshape the story—or the song—toward a more vital and faithful future is an act of deep leadership that offers communities a bold, new identity filled with real hope. By reshaping the story, leaders help a community's identity take on a new form. In the end, people live up to who they think they are, whether as individuals or as congregations. Leaders risk to make the story of who congregations think they are, a better and more faithful story for them to live out than the story of who they have been.

## NOTES

1. Mike Mather, *Sharing Stories, Shaping Community: Vital Ministry in the Small Membership Church* (Nashville: Discipleship Resources, 2002), 16–17.

2. Ibid., 17.

3. Stephen Denning, *The Springboard: How Storytelling Ignites Action in Knowledge-Era Organizations* (Boston: Butterworth Heinemann, 2001), xviii.

4. Ibid., 9–13.

5. Annette Simmons, *The Story Factor* (New York: Basic Books, 2001), 27. Copyright © 2001 by Annette Simmons. Reprinted by permission of Basic Books, a member of Perseus Books Group.

6. Craig Dykstra, "Vision and Leadership," *Initiatives in Religion* 3, no. 1 (Winter 1994), 1–2.

7. Howard Gardner, *Leading Minds: An Anatomy of Leadership* (New York: Basic Books, 1995), 9–11.

8. William Isaacs, *Dialogue and the Art of Thinking Together* (New York: Doubleday, 1999), 252–90.

9. Lawrence Porter and Bernard Mohr, eds., *Reading Book for Human Relations Training* (Arlington, VA: NTL Institute, 1982), 68–71.

10. David A. Roozen and James R. Nieman, eds., *Church, Identity, and Change: Theology and Denominational Structures in Unsettled Times* (Grand Rapids: William B. Eerdmans, 2005), 596.

11. Ronald Heifetz, *Leadership Without Easy Answers* (Cambridge, MA: Belknap Press, 1994).

12. David Bohm, *On Dialogue* (London: Routledge, 1996), 2.

13. Robert D. Pierson, *Needs-Based Evangelism: Become A Good Samaritan Church* (Nashville: Abingdon Press, 2006).

14. J. Gordon Kingsley, "The President as Bard," *AGB Reports*, July/August 1987.

# CHAPTER 3

# Expeditions into What Is Possible

## NARRATIVE LEADERSHIP AND DEEP CHANGE

⌒

### LAWRENCE PEERS

Where Moses stood, "the bush was blazing, yet it was not consumed" (Ex. 3:2). In that holy encounter, he was being summoned into an experience of leadership that he would rather not pursue. After all, he was tending his father-in-law's flock of sheep, minding the task at hand, he didn't need anything else to do. But suddenly, out of nowhere, the Holy Presence calls him to move from the placidity of sheep herding to the seemingly unfathomable task of leading a captive people through an exodus and onto a circuitous journey of liberation. Going from herding sheep to herding people is a tremendous personal shift. Everything in Moses's bones told him he would rather just stay with what he already knew how to do: herding sheep . . . and hiding out!

As religious leaders—clergy and lay alike—we often find ourselves in circumstances not too different from Moses. How often do we prefer the familiar and the safe? How much do we prefer to remain with what is, with no inclination to move toward what is possible? How often as leaders of faith communities do we stay on the edge of our own Red Sea waiting for some miracle to occur before we even budge?

Like Moses, only when we take the plunge of leading do we discover new capacities of self and of faith that were otherwise dormant or underutilized.

## Leading as a New Way of Being

~

Leading change is not just doing something different. It is entering into a new way of being—and from this new way of being can emerge a distinctly new way of leading. That is what Moses's encounter with the blazing bush was all about; it was the beginning of an ontological shift from being a dutiful sheep herder to an empowered leader of a people. Although I doubt that any burning bushes will be appearing on our daily commute from home to office, we too know moments when in order to lead we need to feel called into some qualitatively different ways of being, beyond what is often safe and familiar.

Moving from what is known into a vast uncertainty (the wilderness) with only the slim promise of a new possibility to go toward is all too familiar terrain to any of us attempting to lead change in a congregation.[1] Concurrent with that congregational change is our own journey of change as leaders, which can too often feel like exploring a new territory without a map to guide us.

## Leading Narratively

~

To lead narratively, we leaders must be mindful of the relationship that we choose to have with the congregation's story. Cognitive psychologist Howard Gardner, who has examined the dynamics of leaders, reminds us in *Leading Minds: An Anatomy of Leadership* that "the ultimate impact of the leader depends most significantly on the particular story that he or she relates or embodies, and the receptions to that story on the part of audiences (or collaborators or followers)."[2] How one *embodies a story* is distinct from how one's words *relate a story*. For in embodying a story, we *become* that which we tell; we give a glimpse of what is possible. Such an effort requires us to be mindful of the dynamic tension we then initiate between what is and what can be. Gardner, indeed acknowledges that "the stories of the leaders—be they traditional or novel—must compete with many other extant stories and if the new stories are to succeed, they must transplant, suppress, supplement, or in some measure outweigh the earlier stories, as well as contemporary oppositional counterstories."[3]

Moses not only led the Israelites out of Egypt but also led them to a new understanding of who they were and of what was possible. Along the way Moses too was authoring a new understanding of himself and his role in this pilgrimage of leading a throng of captives into becoming the people of a covenant.

So, we will explore here some practices for leading narratively that are drawn from my applications of narrative therapy to congregational settings. I will illustrate these through case examples from my consulting and coaching practice. Along the way, we will come to understand that as leaders we always have a choice about the relationship we have with the congregation's dominant story about itself. In order to lead, we must be able to honor the story as well as shape the story of the congregation. To lead we must point—in our interactions and in our embodiment of our leadership—to some alternate ways of acting and *ways of being* that hold promise and possibility.

## Navigating Expeditions of What Is Possible

I have found within narrative therapy some insight and guidance for how as leaders we might lead narratively through the uncertain terrain of change and toward new possibilities in our congregations. Michael White, a founder of narrative therapy, in his last book, *Maps of Narrative Practice*, states what can describe our own experiences of leading purposeful change within congregations:

> My lifelong fascination for maps has led me to look at them as a metaphor for my work with people who consult me about a range of concerns, dilemmas, and problems. When we sit down together I know that we are embarking on a journey to a destination that cannot be precisely specified, and via routes that cannot be predetermined. . . . And I know that the adventures to be had on these journeys are not about the confirmation of what is already known, but about expeditions into what is possible for people to know about their lives.[4]

White's remarks, offered before his untimely death, call for some practical directions as we embark on "expeditions into what is possible," not just for the congregations we lead but also for ourselves as leaders. In fact, for us to effect deep change— that is, change that is not just episodic and on the surface but change that is generative and transformative—we need to reauthor our own leadership. In so doing, we are not merely agents of change but, like Moses, we ourselves are changed.

Our leadership role can go through dramatic shifts, not just because of what we *do*, but because of how we *are* in relationship to the congregation's story. As a narrative leader, we may find that if we identify the dominant story of the congregation as a problem-oriented story, we can be tempted to *be* a problem solver. In such a role, we are merely a character in a plot that is already established. Or, we can consciously and intentionally work with the congregation to identify neglected events and exceptions to the dominant story. By linking these yet-to-be-storied events, our role shifts to becoming a composer or coauthor with the congregation of a new story. When we focus the conversation in the congregation on possibilities and new directions, our role shifts to being a midwife to a new vision.

As narrative leaders, we must be aware of what kind of narrators we are—and not only the stories we tell. Do we tend to focus on *what is* and tell the story from the role of a problem solver or rescuer in the story? Or, are we also able to stand outside that story and define our practices as composers, coauthors, or midwives to *what can be*? Obviously, as leaders within a congregation we can't avoid being part of the congregation's story. However, in order to lead we may also need to define ourselves in a different relationship to the dominant story. Let's explore together what that might look like.

## Observing and Not Just Telling the Story

As part of my work in narrative leadership, I often ask leaders of faith communities to acknowledge that they are already swimming in a narrative they have about the congregation. I ask these leaders to imagine this inner chatter, this narrative, as a constant stream of words and sentences that flows through them and around them. Then I instruct them to reach out into this imaginary stream with their hand and randomly snatch a "line" from that inner story that they have about the congregation. As they hold that imaginary line from the story in one hand, I ask them to observe that line. What is that line? What is the mood of that line? How does that line fit into a larger story that they or members have about the congregation? Who else tends to tell this story about the congregation? How does this line typically lead to what comes next in their story? Such a simple (and perhaps ridiculous) exercise makes us aware that even the most random sentences from our inner conversations are fragments of a larger story that a congregation has composed about itself, or that we have participated in composing and sometimes enshrining.

Taking this imaginative exercise one step further, I then ask clergy as they are imaginatively holding the particular line from their story of the congregation, "What is the story about the story you are telling?" Here we recognize that our hermeneutics, our interpretation of the story, usually fits into some larger story that we inherit or embrace. As leaders, we do hold our congregational stories in particular ways. The ways we hold or interpret those stories affect not only what we do but also who we are as characters in that story.

James Hopewell's *Congregations: Stories and Structures* is a classic in the congregational studies field because he claims that some congregations tell a story from a worldview that can be comic, tragic, romantic, or ironic, or some combination of these modes of literature.[5] Hence *the story about the story* makes people aware that the story is headed somewhere, that it is telling something not only about the congregation but also about the worldview of the narrator. What is the genre of the story the leaders tend to tell of the congregation? What is the worldview conveyed in the story you tell or that is told? How does your own worldview compare to that of the congregation? Are you romantics or cynics together? Do you share a comic or a tragic worldview of the events of the congregation? What is the impact of these similar or different worldviews on how you lead?

In a recent gathering of clergy, a pastor realized that she tended to look at all the ways laypeople in her congregation fell short of their commitments. She became what she called a micromanager, creating a great deal of stress in her life and reinforcing her story that "you can't trust lay leaders to follow up." When encouraged to look at the big picture outside her own story, she realized that the story was just as much about her as it was about them. When the lay members didn't follow through, it confirmed her suspicions about laypeople not taking their responsibilities or their faith seriously. Her tendency to be the rescuer and save the day when others didn't follow through made her the hero in her tragic story about them— and about her. When she recognized that her hero or rescuer role was part of her tragic story, she realized she was part of the problem. Desiring to be in a relationship of trust with them, she was open to being coached into a new role that she called "an equipper," as in equipping the saints (Eph. 4:12). From this new narrative, she shifted her perspective of lay leaders and of her own role. She began to see all the ways she could encourage them and pass on skills. She imagined the lay leaders gradually owning their particular way of doing things and of leading.

As she shifted her narrative, her shoulders dropped, her jaw relaxed, her gaze softened. She was embodying her leadership in a new way, right before our eyes. From this new embodiment of her role, she gradually began to realize that there were already exceptions to the story she tended to tell about the lay-people in the congregation. She began to recognize that there were a myriad of ways in which they already did take on responsibilities and do things in their own way, even if it was not her way. These actual, real-life exceptions did not fit into the familiar story she told about them and about herself. Releasing herself from the dilemma of being a rescuer or the hero, she stepped into another story that started a new "expedition into what was possible" for her own leadership. I suspect that something new is happening in the congregation as well.

## Noticing Your Relationship to the Problem-Saturated Story

Often the dominant story that takes hold in congregations in need of deep change is what is known in narrative therapy as the "problem-saturated story," or one in which the focus is on who or what has been going wrong. A problem-saturated story has a momentum of its own. Often, telling the problem-saturated story about the congregational situation has a trance-like effect. The story is reinforcing. People see only those things that reinforce the story. Whatever is contradictory to this story is not seen and therefore goes "unstoried." This type of story can be recognized in a group when someone offers an example of how difficult or awful something is in the congregation, and before you know it, the rest of the group can't help but chime in with more evidence for how truly bad and impossible the situation is. We can almost hear ourselves saying, "You think that's bad? Let me tell you how it is even worse than that!"

Problem-saturated stories have the impact of fact rather than being taken as a narrative crafted by a particular sifting of facts. As leaders we can easily succumb to the power of the problem-saturated story or even become its primary storyteller. For example, I have often noticed in clergy groups that a pastor or rabbi will tell a story about his or her congregation and seek support from others. In response to some well-intentioned advice from colleagues, the clergyperson, who originally asked for help, often goes deeper into why all these suggestions wouldn't work or delves into more shadowy dimensions of the problem story. At this point even the helpers may chime in with sympathetic remarks about how desperate and despairing situations like this—or all congregations—can be.

When we are so immersed in our story about the congregation, we often can't step outside of that story. If we cannot truly observe, we cannot truly lead. Ron Heifetz, author of *Leadership Without Easy Answers*, often talks about this capacity of observing as stepping outside the "dance of activity" in order to take a "balcony perspective." The tools and perspectives of narrative therapy are especially useful in helping clergy begin to get up on "the balcony" and become different observers of their situations, allowing the possibility of different actions and leading to different results.

One modern midrash on Moses's story states, "The miracle may not be that Moses encountered a burning bush, but that he paused long enough to notice it was there."[6] The very shift from being immersed in the dominant story to being a keen observer of the stories that are told, and that we tell, makes us less oblivious as leaders. Who knows how many burning bushes exist within our daily lives as religious leaders, sparking opportunities and possibilities that go unnoticed because we would rather not see them or because we don't see beyond our customary narratives of the congregation.

## Attending to Your Inner Conversation

Moses's task of moving the people of Israel from the familiarity of Egypt, through the massive uncertainty of the wilderness, toward some unknown promised land required him to change his own understanding of himself even as the once-captive people were gaining a new identity and a new way of being.

Such a call to leadership required a significant shift not only in what he was doing but also in Moses's way of being—an ontological shift.[7] Likewise, any deep change has accompanying inner work for ourselves as leaders. Moses's inner work is recorded in Scripture as his list of objections. He claims to be unworthy, he points to his own lack of eloquence, he presents a case for why he should be replaced by someone else. These are only the points recorded in the story. Who knows the myriad ways he may have felt inadequate to the task or what other ways he may have argued that he was not the one to lead.

When we face the prospect of significant change, as religious leaders we may hear echoes of our own voices within Moses's objections. The inner conversations with ourselves or with our God may boil down to "Why me?" or, "Are you sure you have the

right person?" Yet, underlying our case for why we are not up to
the task is a keen understanding that leading change requires
an ontological shift from our present way of being toward a
new way of being and of leading. Like Moses, we may move
toward that ontological shift—kicking and screaming—because it also means that we have to shed our own familiar narrative about ourselves and our congregation.

In my coaching with clergy, many of whom face new leadership challenges, the inner conversations (or stories) they are
having about these challenges are as important as their presentation of what is going on in the congregation. In other words,
the clergyperson's inner changes include shifts in how he or she
observes and not just what he or she is observing. Before we as
religious leaders dare to cross the threshold of leading through
purposeful change, we have to ask ourselves the fundamental questions, "Am I up to it?" and "Am I as a leader willing to
make the shifts I need to make in order to lead?" Only at this
fundamental level of personal reckoning can leaders begin to
embark on the journey of leadership. What we hope will be a
smooth cruise to the promised land can be a long and winding
route through uncertainty, and we need to prepare ourselves
first. The quarreling and grumbling we anticipate among our
congregations as they face deep change can make the Israelites'
incessant grumbling in the wilderness seem like mere singing
in the choir.

## Using Narrative Therapy Approaches
## with Problem-Saturated Stories

Leaders who make the necessary inner shift and stand outside
the dominant, problem-saturated story as an observer will find
that narrative therapy offers a number of techniques that can
help them navigate the change process in the congregation.

These distinctive techniques are far different from the push-pull dynamic that characterizes many congregational change efforts. Rather, they serve as frameworks that can help religious leaders not only avoid some common pitfalls but also shift the conversation in ways that reveal possibilities and directions that might otherwise be obscured.

## Ask Questions that Reveal "Unstoried" Events

One technique narrative leaders can employ with congregations is to identify other stories in the congregation that are often, up to this point, unstoried.

To begin constructing alternatives to the problem-saturated story, I ask questions such as these, adapted from narrative therapy, that often help people get a peek at things outside that particular story:

+ When would you say you do not have the complaint about the congregation?
+ Are there times when the problem is not present?
+ How do you explain the times when the problem is not present?
+ What is different about the times when the complaint is not present?
+ What do you imagine others would say when the complaint is not present?
+ What will be the first sign that things are getting better?

These questions help leaders recognize the dynamic of the problem-focused story in ways that can release them from its mesmerizing effect and allow them to stand outside of it. Other times, by taking on a different point of view, leaders recognize that they have been taking only one of many perspectives as an observer. Shifting the observer can often reveal different actions that are available and different results that are possible.

## Externalize the Problem
## rather than Personalize It

A feature of the problem-saturated story is that it often includes a villain, a problem child, an *unmensch*. The situation becomes personalized in such a way that the message becomes, "If only so-and-so would change, all would be well." In my consulting work, I often hear the phrase "those people" used to refer to those considered "the problem children" in the congregation. A consultant's goal is to help a congregation see its situation systemically, to see how everyone is playing some role in keeping a problem situation intact.

I recently heard a story in one church about a woman who had been so disruptive for so long that the other members of the congregation worked overtime to anticipate questions she might ask in a congregational meeting in order to avoid conflict with her. After more than a decade of this, and under the guidance of a new leader, they finally recognized that a disruptive person in a congregation is kept in place by those who, often with good intentions, tolerate this sort of behavior until it is no longer bearable. By using questions from the narrative approach, such as those above, congregations and their leaders begin to see that the person is not the problem, the problem is the problem—and, indeed, it is their relationship to the problem that is the problem.

A recent training session I led with a group of rabbis illustrates this shift toward changing one's relationship to the problem. In this training, a new rabbi mentioned how he felt he was being blamed for the fact that in his congregation they could not gather a minyan (a group of at least ten) for evening prayers. The rabbi explained that he was doing his part—he showed up as one of the ten. He called members and asked for their commitment to attend. Invariably, not enough folks showed up, and those who had gathered resented taking the time or felt annoyed at those who did not keep their promises.

Even if they did not explicitly blame the rabbi for the low commitment, he often felt they did.

In the conversation with the rabbi, I shifted the focus from who was to blame (which is often an endless cycle leading nowhere) to an externalizing conversation in which, as Michael White says, "the problem is the problem." An externalizing conversation, according to White, includes describing the problem using the "parlance of the people seeking therapy and that is based on their understanding of life."[8] Consequently, in this interaction, I picked up on the rabbi's language and began to talk with the rabbi about the "not enough commitment" problem. This allowed us to depersonalize the problem and to begin to talk about the situations in which not enough commitment is present. Then we explored the effects of the problem on the synagogue, on the rabbi, on the people in the synagogue, and so forth. In narrative therapy this is called "mapping the effects of the problem." From there we could evaluate whether the effects of this problem were welcome or not, and if not, why not.

As our conversation proceeded, we realized that there were indeed times that the not-enough-commitment problem was not present, such as on high holy days, at memorial services, and especially at family events. We then talked about what was present in these alternate exceptions to the problem circumstances. The rabbi was able to see that people found something meaningful in these events; or that generations of commitment and loyalty supported people in making the commitment to those events in which they did show up. By looking at the exceptions, he saw that he could refocus his efforts on the alternate story—that is, what contributes to the not-enough-commitment problem not being present in the life of the synagogue.

Because the rabbi not only stood outside of the problem but also took on the role of a different observer of the situation, he saw a whole range of new actions that could lead to some new results that built upon what people actually valued. He

discovered more possibilities for how he could lead and what
he could teach.

## Construct an Alternate Story

Once people can externalize the problem they are facing, often
they are also freed up to recognize more of the situation than
is usually permitted in typical discourses about "what's wrong
with this congregation." In externalizing conversations, often a
new kind of conversation begins to emerge. These "reauthoring conversations," White explains, "invite people to continue
to develop and tell stories about their lives, but they also help
people to include some of the more neglected but potentially
significant events and experiences that are 'out of phase' with
their dominant storylines. These events and experiences can be
considered 'unique outcomes' or 'exceptions.'"[9]

I worked with one congregation badly in need of redevelopment, given that its membership was graying and its endow-
ment was shrinking. Congregation members told the story of
how every time they tried some growth initiative it would be
met with an effort by some members to sabotage or undermine
it. Consequently, they felt caught and at an impasse. The image
that emerged in our conversations was that they had a "finger-
trap problem." They had a tendency to pull in opposite directions when change occurred—and this kept them trapped,
much like the child's toy known as a finger trap.[10]

We focused on the effects of this finger-trap problem and
mapped the effects of this problem on their faith community,
on its capacity to grow, and on its ability to initiate change. Congregants readily agreed that they did not like the effects of this
recurring problem because it kept the congregation trapped,
preventing it from moving forward, and the experience became
painful over time. People tended to stay in their factions, react-
ing to each other and finding the push and pull more engaging
than the effort to pull in the same direction.

We then explored all the times in the congregation's life when the finger-trap problem was not present. We looked at what people were *doing* as a congregation during the times when the finger-trap problem was not prevalent. White calls this mapping the "landscape of action."[11] One example was the time the church's youth organized a benefit for the victims of the 2006 tsunami disaster. Without exception, members of the church supported their efforts, even when the youth were promoting music and inviting people to the church that did not fit the congregation's stereotyped understanding of itself. People in the congregation worked together in spite of their differences. The event was successful not only as a fundraiser but also as an event in which the congregation acted as a whole. This was an example of the congregation *pulling together* in the same direction, an exception to its finger-trap problem.

"What would the youth of this church, who saw you as a congregation act so readily and cooperatively in their fundraising project, say about you as a congregation?" I asked. This and other reauthoring questions helped congregants see that an alternate story was possible, and that the dynamics of the alternate story about the congregation were different than the dominant, problem-saturated story about the congregation they had held in the past.

## Describing New Possibilities

In the time of the Babylonian exile of the Jewish people, the prophet Jeremiah could have commiserated with the problem-saturated story of a people who were in despair, far from home, and in captivity once again. Instead, he spoke the prophetic word: "Build houses and live in them; plant gardens and eat what they produce. Take wives and have sons and daughters; take wives for your sons, and give your daughters in marriage, that they may bear sons and daughters; multiply there, and do not decrease. But seek the welfare of the city where I have sent you into exile, and pray to the LORD on its behalf, for in its welfare you will find your welfare" (Jer. 29:5–7).

In essence Jeremiah was saying, "Don't cave in to your sense of despair and hopelessness." He reminded them who they were outside of the problem and encouraged them to do what they knew how to do when they were not in exile: plant gardens, start families, and promote the well-being of the place where they dwelled. These actions were the start of a new story. Jeremiah was prophetically helping the people of Israel reauthor their story in the midst of exile.

The psalmist ponders, "But how could we sing a song of the LORD in a foreign land?" As religious leaders, we too ponder how we can sing in the midst of turmoil. A narrative leader must dare to be as prophetic as Jeremiah. Even in the midst of trouble or uncertainty, as narrative leaders we must be able to help others stand outside the mesmerizing effects of the problem-saturated story. As narrative leaders, we must be resilient and resourceful enough to resist internalizing the situation. By recognizing that the problem is the problem, as leaders we can facilitate a conversation that studies with curiosity the dynamic effects of this problem on the health, capacities, and faithfulness of the congregation.

Shifting the congregation's relationship to the problem comes only when its members can examine these effects and deeply and resoundingly say, "No, we don't want to continue with these effects of the problem." A narrative leader uses questions to help point a congregation toward the possibilities and directions inherent in a situation but often obscured by people's usual problem-saturated and personalizing approaches to the situation. As narrative leaders we provoke the alternate story by asking, "What would you like instead? Where would you like to be headed?" "What would be the first sign that we are moving in the new direction?" Then a threshold to a new possibility for the congregation emerges.

The cumulative effect of this process, rather than a dead end, is a congregational conversation of possibilities. Margaret Wheatley, in her book *Turning to One Another*, underlines the role of leaders in creating powerful conversations that can promote deep change: "There is no power greater than a community discovering what it cares about. Ask, 'What's possible?' not 'What's wrong?' Keep asking. . . . Be brave enough to start a conversation that matters."[12] Narrative leaders lead expeditions into what is possible by their willingness to elicit alternate, generative stories that point to possibilities more than problems. In so doing, they shift their ways of being a leader and the congregation's way of being.

## NOTES

1. Gilbert R. Rendle, *Leading Change in the Congregation: Spiritual and Organizational Tools for Leaders* (Herndon, VA: Alban Institute, 1998).

2. Howard Gardner, *Leading Minds: An Anatomy of Leadership* (New York: Basic Books, 1995), 14.

3. Ibid.

4. Michael White, *Maps of Narrative Practice* (New York: W. W. Norton, 2007), 6.

5. James F. Hopewell, *Congregations: Stories and Structures* (Philadelphia: Fortress Press, 1987).

6. A paraphrase from Marc Gellman's *Does God Have a Big Toe? Stories About Stories in the Bible* (New York: Harper Collins, 1989).

7. Alan Seiler, *Coaching to the Human Soul: Ontological Coaching and Deep Change*, vol. 1 (Victoria, Australia: Newfield Australia, 2005).

8. Michael White, *Maps of Narrative Practice* (New York: W. W. Norton, 2007), 41.

9. White, *Maps of Narrative Practice*, 61.

10. Also known as a Chinese finger trap or Mexican handcuffs.

11. White, *Maps of Narrative Practice*, 99–100.

12. Margaret J. Wheatley, *Turning to One Another: Simple Conversations to Restore Hope to the Future* (San Francisco: Berrett-Koehler, 2002).

# CHAPTER 4

# Place-Based Narratives

## AN ENTRY POINT FOR
## MINISTRY TO THE SOUL OF A COMMUNITY

⁓

## ALICE MANN

While other essays in this volume focus on the way stories live and breathe *inside* congregations, this chapter aims to take our discussion of narrative leadership for a walk around the neighborhood, a drive along the freeway. Each congregation's story evolves within a specific geographic, social, and narrative setting. Like other institutions in postindustrial society, the congregation is part of this local ecology whether it chooses to notice or not.

Congregations are born from a generative spark of interaction between stories of faith and stories of place. Some person or group looks out on a particular landscape and says, "There should be a church—or there should be a congregation of our preferred type—in this particular community." That conclusion is not, of course, an isolated thought but part of a larger narrative that has shaped the awareness of the founder or founding group, a story about "who we are" (cultural and religious identity), "what we are called to do or be" (religious purpose), and "where we are now" (community and cultural context). Throughout the history of a congregation, narratives of faith and narratives of place collide and converge, compartmentalize and connect in many and changing ways.

Congregations that take cognizance of and responsibility for their ecological relationships will have a deeper, more grounded ministry. Even the congregation that is regional in scope and highly associational in style is still part of the physical, social, and narrative web of those communities where the building is situated and where its members live, work, and play. As congregations explore the intersection between their own core narratives and those of their local community or communities, new possibilities for—and even new categories of—ministry and mission may emerge. Specifically, congregations may discover new ways to interact intentionally and redemptively with the narrative life of the places they inhabit.

Over the last few years, I have become interested in place-based narratives as a powerful component of personal, civic, and congregational life. This awareness and curiosity did not arise in a vacuum; I myself had moved to a new place in 2002. Though I have changed residence quite a few times in my adult life, this last move has special significance for me. That meaning is captured in a remark I recall from an address by poet and social critic Wendell Berry. It is good, he said, for the young to leave home and explore the wider world, but at some point it is important to stop and say, "This is it, this will be home."[1] The seeds of significance and commitment that were present at the time of my move sprouted with surprising urgency during a sabbatical summer in 2005; in the stillness that summer allowed me, I experienced an almost physical ache to know and work with other citizens, to help make this city a good place to live. So my attraction to the subject of place-based narratives arises at the intersection of at least three personal story lines: a quest story about finding and claiming a home place; a discernment story (common during sabbaticals) about addressing vocational restlessness and scratching the itch for some new departure in my professional life; and the palpable narrative force of this place itself as it works on my imagination.

As a result, I have come to believe that the questions "Where am I?" and "What is happening here?" are among the most profound questions individuals can pose. In congregational planning and discernment, this vocabulary of place or location is often used metaphorically. "Where are we now?" may be a figurative way of asking what steps the congregation has completed in a planning process, how far the congregation has progressed in a size transition, or how close the capital campaign has come to meeting its goal. In this discussion, I want to wake up these dozing metaphors of place and refocus on their immediate and physical meanings. In doing so, I am joining a particular conversation about the significance of place for postindustrial society and for faith communities, and I am building upon an existing vocabulary of relations between congregation and context.

## The Changing Meanings of Place

The mobility of the U.S. population is a familiar idea. Census 2000 found that about 60 percent of U.S. residents still lived in the state where they were born, down from about 64 percent in 1980.[2] In any given year, about one in seven people were expected to move. About half of them would probably stay in the same county and about one-fifth move out of state. The likelihood of a move in any given year was shown to be dramatically affected by age; if you were in your twenties, the chances would be one in three, while for those over age sixty-five, the chances would be only one in twenty. The likelihood of moving was also shown to differ markedly by the type of residence you occupied: one in three renters was expected to move each year while only one in fourteen homeowners would typically do so. Since the publication of this data from Census 2000, changes have been observed in mobility patterns due both to long-term trends and to the sudden economic downturn in the fall of 2008. Tracking the longer-term trends, the Pew Research

Center reported a steady decline in mobility due to factors such
as an aging population and the rise of two-career couples; and
in April 2009, the U.S. Census Bureau reported that recent
economic difficulties had caused mobility to decline even further (at least temporarily) to 1962 levels.[3]

While the tide seems to have shifted in recent years, high
mobility has interacted with generational differences, house-
hold economics, and land-use patterns to reduce people's
overall sense of identification and involvement with specific
communities. A report in 2000 by Robert Putnam and his
colleagues at the Saguaro Seminar, a program at the Kennedy
School of Government, characterized the situation as a "downward spiral of civic apathy" driven by the impending loss of an
"exceptionally civic generation of older Americans" and the "far
less civic-minded" attitudes of those born between 1946 and
1980, plus "two-career families, urban sprawl, and television."[4]
The generational rotation theory of Strauss and Howe predicts
that the Millennial generation, just hitting young adulthood,
will manifest greater group-mindedness and community concern than seen in recent generational cohorts. But in the mean-
time, a variety of countermovements are emerging that seek to
establish a new sense of place in a global age.[5]

Across the country, in university departments of geography,
architecture, regional planning, and political science, teachers,
authors, and practitioners are making the case for a new commitment to place. One eloquent advocate is political scientist
Timothy Beatley: "We fundamentally *need* places, and in this
increasingly global epoch this need is more critical than ever
before. We need meaningful places to improve the quality of
our lives and the depth and meaning of our personal and interpersonal relationships. Indeed, the planet needs such places
for its very sustenance and survival. . . . Sustaining *place* helps
us create *sustainable* places."[6] Thinking like this lies behind creative movements in environmental design, green building, par-
ticipatory community planning, habitat restoration, and smart
growth approaches to zoning and land use.

Place is reasserting itself in other disciplines as well, such as conflict transformation and peacemaking. Urging practitioners to avoid imprisonment in scientific and mechanistic thought patterns, conflict transformation specialist John Paul Lederach issues a challenge to his colleagues to root their work in discerning "the soul of place." He describes this as a journey to "locate *who* I am in the particular place and *what* is the nature of this place *where* I am located.... Approach the context with care and respect. Walk carefully. Watch and listen to those who know the setting. Do not presume to know solutions or to provide preconceived recipes. Understand yourself as part of the larger whole."[7]

Lederach notes that soul of place can seem like a very strange idea, as people are far more accustomed to talking about the place of soul as the place in their lives occupied by meaning or faith or spirit. In contrast, he describes the soul of place as a "kind of inner voice [of the place itself] that speaks to each of us personally, calling out to understand the nature of the place where we find ourselves and the nature of our place in that location."[8] By doing so, we might avoid becoming perpetrators of mindless violence toward a living web of relations (both past and present) that constitute a place. We might steer away from the technocratic imperialism that treats each place as an example of general principles already defined rather than as an autonomous and mysterious self to be discovered.

In the arena of Christian spirituality, teacher and author Parker Palmer has implicitly argued for the importance of reconnecting with place in his discussion of public relationships, which occupy a crucial mediating position between people's private lives and the political or governmental arena. The public life, he says, "involves strangers who come together without elaborate institutional mechanisms—in taxis, on streetcorners, at museums and sidewalk cafes . . . encountering each other with no political agenda at all. In fact, the public life is 'prepolitical.' It is more basic than politics; it existed long before political institutions were developed and refined; and a healthy [democratic] political process . . . depends on the preexistence of a healthy public life."[9]

Palmer notes that the search for spiritual growth or personal healing becomes profoundly distorted and narcissistic in the absence of a rich fabric of public relationships to provide balance, energy, and outside perspective. At the same time, weakness in this local fabric of relations turns larger political and governmental processes into spectator sports. While Palmer's public life can be conducted in the transient settings of postindustrial society—at least by the person willing to pull out the earpiece and engage the taxi driver as a fellow human being—it can only flourish in more sustained involvement with a specific place. College students and church volunteers get a taste of these possibilities when they go on mission trips to New Orleans or to a village in Guatemala, settings that convey a more distinctive sense of place than the typical U.S. city or suburb. Perhaps such pilgrimages have their greatest effect when they cause participants to notice, and engage with, the web of public relationships already and potentially present in the places they actually inhabit.

## Models of Congregational Relations with Place

Much of my day-to-day work involves congregational strategic planning and visioning stimulated variously by community growth pressures, congregational decline, leadership transitions, conflict, or the yearning to discover a clearer and more compelling call. Lederach's key questions can be applied to the congregation as a whole—Who are we in this particular place and what is the nature of this *place* where we are located?—and figure prominently in such strategic work. Indeed, one might define a strategic choice as one that arises from the core mission, *takes account of the context*, and focuses the resources of the whole system on a few central matters. While context includes more than place, the dynamics of locality remain a critical factor for the vast majority of congregations.

Often, congregations are only dimly aware of the relationship they are living out with the places they and their members inhabit. The congregation's historic positioning (as a pillar of community life or a neighborhood church, for example) may be taken for granted in spite of shifting dynamics. Discussions of place may be confined to an outreach committee whose leaders are working with a fairly limited definition of what community ministry can mean (for example, collecting food and toiletries, spending a night at the homeless shelter, or joining a Habitat for Humanity build—all excellent things to do). Rarely do congregational leaders spend much time asking, "Who *are* we to this town (or city or county)?" or "What is the deep character of this place (locality), and how might God be calling us to contribute to that character?" Nevertheless, the congregation is always living out some kind of story about place, always enacting some kind of relationship—consciously or unconsciously—with the local ecology. To raise awareness about such relationships, and how they differ from congregation to congregation, consultants sometimes sketch out conceptual models for leaders to reflect upon. Below I describe a few frameworks that are often used to expand the congregation's vocabulary of relations with place: parish and commuter churches, bonding and bridging social capital, garden plots and far fields, mission trajectories, religious presence, congregational self-image, and religious ecology.[10]

## Parish and Commuter Churches

For decades sociologists of religion have described two contrasting models of interaction with place that a congregation may be living out. Geographically defined congregations have often been called parishes while more associational faith communities (sometimes called commuter churches) draw people across geographical boundaries based on their similarities in ethnicity, class, doctrinal leanings, or preference for a particular style of religious expression. The parish terminology usually occurs in denominations with a memory of having been the established church, either in the "old country" or here in the North America (Congregationalists in Massachusetts and Anglicans in Virginia, for example). Generally, only the established or dominant faith tradition could claim the right to create fixed boundaries and direct adherents to participate in an assigned congregation. Within U.S. Protestantism (and particularly among Episcopalians and Lutherans), continuing use of the term *parish* may sometimes imply a heightened emphasis on geography in shaping the congregation's identity and purpose, but even these denominations have a highly associational dynamic today. In the 1950s, Episcopalians often passed by the nearest church to get to one with the "right" liturgical style, either "lower" or "higher" than the church nearby. And in the 1970s, the same families might have become pilgrims again, seeking to find or avoid a "charismatic" church. Likewise, Roman Catholic parishes may find it difficult to prevent adherents from attaching themselves to the congregation whose liturgical style, building, or priest they prefer.

## Bonding and Bridging Social Capital

More recently, scholars such as Robert Putnam have noted differences in the dominant type of social capital—that is, networks and practices of affiliation—that bring people together, whether in civic institutions or in congregations.[11] Where bonding is the salient pattern, the institution is most effective at gathering people based on their similarities and at building relational ties through common purposes and activities. Where bridging prevails, the institution typically brings together dissimilar people and groups who are pursuing diverse projects. Bridging can occur vertically (up and down the ladder of class or social position) or horizontally (across racial, ethnic, or religious lines). While some have argued that parish congregations inherently serve the bridging function, and so generate more social capital in their geographic area, others, like Nancy Ammerman, point out the degree to which associational churches with "strong, face-to-face communities, fortified by spiritual strength [generate] social capital."[12]

## Garden Plots and Far Fields

In an environment where ties to place have been weakened, congregations are faced with new questions about the way they will undertake their social mission, often called outreach by mainline Protestants. Building on the work of Putnam and others, demographer Anthony Healy lifts up two models congregations might consider. In his "garden plots" model, congregations act as a "bridge among different people within a place as the basis of developing social missions." In his "far fields" model, "the power of bonding [is] the basis for undertaking tasks to which the congregation feels drawn, tasks that are not boundaried by place."[13] Healy's far fields description awoke in me a memory of my first job out of college. I worked for the Metropolitan Christian Council of Philadelphia, where I met people from many denominations. I recall sitting in a committee meeting with a Quaker who remarked that he had made a lifelong commitment to work on the issue of prison reform—a comment that made a deep impression on me. Looking back, I suspect that the Friends Meeting he attended was a small and dedicated group of people whose spiritual practices fostered in him and in others the compassion, courage, and staying power to pay attention to an unpopular cause. Prisons, and the policies that govern them, were and still are far fields, indeed, for most congregations.

## Mission Trajectories

The Percept Group, a source of demographic studies for churches, identifies four ministry trajectories—town, regional, magnet, and mission—that arise from the interaction of population density and population diversity in the surrounding community.[14] The *town* congregation, whose setting is low density and low diversity, only has to be—like Lake Wobegon Lutheran—a pretty good church in order to function effectively within its environment. When the town of Lake Wobegon is overtaken by suburban sprawl, however, a *regional* dynamic emerges that favors congregations with high quality programs and critical mass of, say, at least two-hundred-fifty people in worship and church school attendance per Sunday. In more intensely urbanized areas, high density and high diversity make it hard for a town concept of ministry—"We welcome everybody"—to flourish. Instead, a *magnet* trajectory, with a sharply defined audience and the communication channels to reach them, tends to fit the context better. Finally, in settings of low density but high diversity—Alaska, for example—a *mission* trajectory will recognize that conventional models of congregational life (such as a church with a building and a seminary-trained pastor) can only be sustained with ongoing outside support.

### Four Ministry Trajectories

|                | HIGH DENSITY | LOW DENSITY |
|----------------|--------------|-------------|
| LOW DIVERSITY  | Regional     | Town        |
| HIGH DIVERSITY | Magnet       | Mission     |

## Religious Presence

In an important study from the 1980s, church sociologists David Roozen, William McKinney, and Jackson Carroll mapped out four distinctive "varieties of religious presence" that can help us understand some of the different ways congregations relate to place.[15] Some congregations see their presence largely in terms of providing sacred space that serves as a safe haven from this world (the *sanctuary* orientation). Others see themselves as actively involved in seeking individuals who need salvation and thereby changing the world one person at a time (the *evangelistic* orientation). Still others see themselves as promoters and preservers of what is good in the world (the *civic* orientation), while the last group seeks to change the structures of the world that cause suffering and injustice (the *activist* congregation).[16]

More recent studies by sociologists Penny Edgell Becker, Arthur Farnsley II, and colleagues have added the idea of the "family-support" or "customer service" congregation that provides full-service programming for members and their families.[17] While most congregations will express more than one of these orientations, congregations that embrace a dominant orientation tend to produce a clearer church identity and to reduce the number of conflicts about the "right" way of pursuing mission. I work with many churches, for example, whose historic identity is strongly *civic*, emphasizing the formation of individual conscience in their members while carefully avoiding congregational positions on controversial issues. When clergy, lay leaders, or denominational officials propose that these churches take a more *activist* approach by voting on a hot-button issue, deep resistance may arise—and may be misinterpreted as evidence of members' conservatism on the issue itself rather than as a signal that the approach is inconsistent with the congregation's existing mission orientation.

## Congregational Self-Image

In the 1990s, research by church sociologists Carl Dudley and Sally Johnson generated a fresh vocabulary to portray a spectrum of congregation-community relationships. Dudley and Johnson describe the congregation's primary role and self-image within its local context as "pillar, pilgrim, prophet, survivor, or servant."[18] Dudley notes that this list of congregational self-images can be subdivided into two "turf types," depending on whether the congregation understands itself as ministering to its immediate community or to a larger region.[19] These roles may shift or mix for an individual congregation. The ethnically oriented *pilgrim* church, for example, may change location freely in its early years but may later come to occupy a more settled place in one particular community and to enact a *pillar* role.

## Religious Ecology

Also in the 1990s, sociologist Nancy Ammerman led a large and comprehensive study that resulted in a landmark book titled *Congregation and Community*.[20] Ammerman identified subgroups of congregations, discernible across the entire national landscape, that responded in distinctive ways to changes in their surrounding communities, including the following:

+ Moving to a location more favorable to the congregation's current style and demographics;
+ Adapting the ministry emphasis (programs, culture, demographic reach) to new realities in the community;
+ Keeping, and perhaps even reinforcing, one key ministry emphasis but drawing from a wider region (niche ministry);
+ Starting a new congregation from scratch within the facilities of a church that has died;
+ Keeping things the same, as far as possible, even if this means that the congregation will probably cease within the foreseeable future.

One member of Ammerman's research team, Nancy Eiesland, went on to make a different application of the concept of religious ecology.[21] In her own study, Eiesland focused on the whole array of religious congregations that coexist within a *single* community landscape and how they affect one another as they respond in various ways to community change.

## Attending to Place through Local Stories

Whatever vocabulary may be used to illuminate a congregation's fundamental role, identity, and orientation with respect to the place it inhabits, Lederach's underlying questions, which I have adapted to apply to entire congregations, demand attention:

+ Who or what have *we* been to this place (this local community, however we define it)? What has been our distinctive role, niche, or position within the web of this local ecology?
+ What is the distinctive character, personality, or soul of this *place*? What are its gifts and its besetting sins? Where is its struggle about identity and purpose occurring right now, and what is at stake?
+ What is God's *call* to us today in our relationship to this place?

As a congregation ponders its own sense of identity and purpose, and its community's soul or character, stories should be given center stage. To some extent, this already happens. It is not unusual today for a congregation at a key developmental turning point, such as a pastoral transition or a major visioning process, to revisit and reexamine its own history—that is, to retell its own story to itself. Unfortunately, this is often done in a perfunctory way, assuming that everyone knows the story and understands what its lessons are for the present moment. When congregational history telling is done well, the congregation gives careful attention to the following:

+ Gathering a good mix of participants (ages, life circumstances, tenures in the congregation, tenures in the local community)

+ Eliciting lively *oral* versions of the church's story from all participants and preventing the group from running prematurely to a book or an "official" church historian

+ Mapping (usually on a long, continuous band of paper on the wall) the parallel streams of history—what was going on in the local community and the wider culture in each era; what was going on in the congregation itself; and what was happening in the lives of the people in the room (including a note of the year when each started participating in the church's life)

+ Exploring differing versions of the story being told by different people and subgroups, with the assumption that the congregation needs to learn something from each version, even if the differing accounts will never be completely reconciled

+ Asking people to articulate the meaning of this multilayered story *for their church today.* (Since many people do not understand that history is a continuing process of reconsideration, congregations usually need encouragement to make their own current interpretation—even of well-worn narratives.)

+ Looking ahead to the next chapter in the congregation's story as one that will be coauthored (like all that has come before) by God and human beings. A good guiding question might be, "If we are responsive to what God has done in the past and to God's leading right now, what might the next chapter look like?"

These are excellent practices and worthy of emulation. However, I would argue that Lederach's second question, "What is the distinctive character, personality, or *soul* of this place?" usually gets little attention. If one is listening closely, the character or soul of this place is probably being reflected in some way in the stories people are telling and (perhaps more powerfully) in the style, genre, or tone in which they are told.[22] But rarely, in my experience, does a congregation spend much time discerning the soul—the inner life—of the place in which it ministers or relating its own vocation to the spiritual possibilities and struggles of its local community. Today my own thinking and research is largely focused on this question: *How can a congregation use place-based narratives as entry points for redemptive interaction with the soul of the place it inhabits?* The following discussion of place-based narratives is meant to provide a starting place for any and all who identify with this endeavor.

## What Are Place-Based Narratives?

Place-based narratives are shared, persistent, and dynamic stories people commonly tell about "here." While one could look at narratives of place at a completely individual level, I use the term *place-based narratives* to mean the stories that are *shared* within the community context, those that may be referenced in civic life through commemorative events, memorial structures, newspaper articles, library displays, and the rhetoric of local controversies. The focus is also on *persistent* stories that have remained active in the public imagination over time and on *dynamic* stories that are called into service in a variety of ways and assigned new meanings as circumstances change.[23]

Place-based narratives always accomplish certain tasks. First, they give "here" a name—a powerful act, to be sure. The title people bestow on their place defines a narrative space, a special little world. This power of naming came to my attention when I moved to my current home in Haverhill, Massachusetts, a city of sixty thousand people located about an hour north of Boston. My house is situated in a leafy old neighborhood called Bradford. When people ask me where I live, I usually say, "Haverhill—one of the old mill cities along the Merrimack Valley." My neighbor, on the other hand, always says his home is in Bradford and describes himself as living in the suburbs. These place names and definitions locate us within different narrative frameworks, connect us with different channels of information, assign significance to different events, and lead us to connect with our (apparently shared) environment in markedly different ways.

Second, place-based narratives provide "here" with a trajectory that stretches over time. They sketch out the remembered past—who came here first and from where, what used to be here that the community is proud of or pining for, what tragedies have occurred here that have marked people's memories, and which notable personalities have left their imprint on local life. These narratives describe the place's present reality—who lives here today and what they are like; what is changing now, for better or for worse; and what forces are affecting lives in the community. And they outline imagined futures—the paths of progress or development; the trends of breakdown and demolition (physical and social) that people seek to resist or to hasten; and the potential shape of the common life in years to come.

Finally, a shared narrative of place gives rise to a common field of concerns, possibilities, and relationships. Social theorists have begun to borrow from physics the concept of a field of forces (such as gravitational, electrical, or magnetic) to describe change and movement that cannot be accounted for by a visible, proximate force. Comparing one place to another, different patterns, tendencies, and habits of interaction and development become evident. One major unseen force is the story a community tells about itself. It is not the slick, promotional version on the Chamber of Commerce website but the grassroots version of the story, the one people tell each other to explain and comment upon important happenings or controversial proposals.

As a newcomer to my own community of Haverhill, Massachusetts, I have noticed a thread of shared narrative about urban renewal efforts of the late 1960s, stories told in a tone that ranges from cynicism to fury. The story conveys how some anonymous *they* tore down the fabric of whole neighborhoods, encouraged by the incentive of federal funding to remove "blighted" areas. What a newcomer sees today is a wide swath of land—cutting right across the key entry point to downtown—where the nineteenth-century street grid has been demolished and subsequently replaced by a suburban-style strip mall, several concrete multistory apartment blocks, and a large new police station. While those structures may serve important functions, the city appears to suffer very real pain, akin to what an amputee feels from a phantom limb. Weekly "Remember When" photos in the local newspaper frequently include scenes of what used to be in this urban renewal zone. In civic conversation, one senses that the soul of Haverhill—forty years later—is still grieving its remembered past and still skeptical of any plan for improvement. This soul condition creates a force field of nostalgia, resentment, and cynicism about change that drags down efforts to build quality and consensus in present-day plans and possibilities.

While place-based narratives are intensely local and idiosyncratic, they always participate in larger stories—metanarratives—of change, development, or growth. The term *urban renewal* was commonly used to invoke and advance a powerful metanarrative about U.S. cities, and its vocabulary (including words like *blight* and *renewal*) was symbolically charged. Metanarratives often function on this mythic level, gaining their power from archetypal resonance. Certain artifacts from the religious history of the Americas serve as examples of powerful, overarching story lines. The Puebloan kivas of the Southwest once embodied (and still do for Native American populations) a powerful metanarrative of emergence from the earth. The seventeenth-century clapboard meetinghouse in a New England town evolved from, then further nurtured, a metanarrative of pilgrimage to a promised land—a place destined to be claimed, renamed, and "civilized" according to specific religious ideals. Today the mall and the megachurch at the big highway interchange participate in a particular metanarrative of social and economic development, with an emphasis on mobility, individual choice, and the abundant provision of culturally attractive products and programs. Place-based narratives—both the local particulars and the metanarratives of change and growth—are key elements in the cultural toolkit that a community of people employs to make sense of the world.[24]

As I have already illustrated with the story of urban redevelopment in Haverhill, a new resident to a particular locale will notice certain events and eras that are referenced repeatedly by different voices in a variety of settings. Over time the newcomer gains an impression of the meanings commonly attached to these events and the uses made of them. A few years into my tenure in Haverhill, I began to piece together the details of one especially potent and troublesome story from our community's founding era—called by one local writer "the most famous incident that occurred in the 350 years of Haverhill history."[25] This story, I have learned, became one of the first pieces of narrative literature produced in the English colonies, and—from its earliest written versions—fused a story of faith with a story of place. While this particular story may be older and more dramatic than founding-era stories from many other communities, my intent in sharing it is to suggest the rich potential of narrative inquiry and stimulate curiosity about the place your congregation inhabits.

# A Provocative Narrative of Place

At the time of its founding in 1640, the settlement called Haverhill, located at the northwest frontier of the Massachusetts Bay Colony, had peaceful interactions with the Pennacook tribe, which had occupied this parcel of land along the Merrimack River. By 1697, however, competition between the French and English for New World dominance had erupted into King William's War, one of a series of conflicts in which Canadian Indian tribes allied with the French conducted raids on English settlements.

In March 1697, a Haverhill woman named Hannah Duston was kidnapped during such a raid, along with her newborn daughter and her daughter's nurse. As the raiding party was leaving the settlement, an Indian brave dashed her infant daughter's head against a tree. Hannah and the nurse, plus a youth captured in a different raid, were taken north along the river to Contoocook Island, where they were guarded by an Indian family of twelve. In the middle of the night, Hannah awakened the other two settlers and led them in an attack on their captors, using the Indians' own tomahawks. They killed two warriors, two women, and six children; scalped the dead; then set off for home in an Indian canoe. Among the Indian family, only one badly injured woman and one boy escaped.

Cotton Mather swiftly transformed this story into a sermon that same year, followed five years later by a longer tract, one of the very first pieces of narrative literature produced in colonial America.[26] In Mather's hands, raw and morally complicated events were given highly allegorical and controlled religious meanings. According to historian Robert Arner:

> Mather is not one to raise moral objections to the slaughter of sleeping Indians. His Biblical allusions [to Jael, from

the book of Judges, for example] simultaneously provide
him with a moral framework to justify Hannah's deed and a
means of placing her exploits in an epic context related to the
national destiny of the Puritan people. She emerges from this
narrative as a seventeenth-century savior of her nation, her
heroism unquestionably a model to be emulated. Thus inter-
preted, transformed, and justified, she passed into the hands
of nineteenth-century New England writers, who slowly began to alter her image.[27]

Arner notes that the power and popularity of this story were
demonstrated by its inclusion in many books of New England
tales and its widely divergent interpretations by major authors
such as John Greenleaf Whittier (*Legends of New England*),
Nathaniel Hawthorne ("The Duston Family"), and Henry
David Thoreau (*A Week on the Concord and Merrimack Riv-
ers*). Having evolved initially from a captive's account into a
religious treatise, then successively from a tale for school children to an ethical conundrum to a mist-enshrouded myth,
the Hannah Duston story disappeared from the mainstream
of American folklore in the middle of the nineteenth century.
Noting that Thoreau was the last major author to deal with
this story, Arner explains: "Hannah is emphatically not a feminine charmer like Pocahontas, nor does she reflect the American character."[28]

I interpret this last comment to mean that Hannah Duston
did not—after a certain point in history—fit the nation's self-
perception. Whether she reflects the actual character of the
nation is a deeper question. Historian Richard Slotkin sees colonial leaders using captivity stories like Hannah Duston's to
work out, and justify, their antagonistic relationship with the
wild, including both the untamed physical environment and
the various indigenous human populations of North America.[29] Campaigns over the next two centuries to subjugate or
eradicate Native American populations were just as successful

(and undoubtedly seemed just as necessary to the American project) as Duston's counterattack. And today's controversies about the way the United States relates to enemies—debates about preemptive attacks, justifications for torture, the rights of wartime captives—take us back to the same longstanding issues of national character raised in the Hannah Duston narratives.

While Duston's story lost its prominence in the literature and folklore of the United States after the Civil War, it retained a central and iconic status among narratives of place in the Merrimack Valley. In June 1874 a statue of Duston was dedicated on Contoocook Island—possibly the first permanent monument erected in the United States to honor the heroism of a real woman. The stone figure is shown holding a tomahawk in her right hand and a bundle of scalps in her left. One of the monument's key promoters was local historian and poet Robert B. Caverly, whose dedication speech richly expresses (even as it attempts to lay to rest) the ambiguities of the remembered events:

> Since then [1697], sad to relate, the entire race of red men in New-England . . . have vanished away. This, indeed, came to pass, partly through the aggressive intrusions of English settlers, oft repeated; partly through the cruel interference of the Canadian French, who tainted the tribes; yet mostly, perhaps, through the inordinate, unbridled infirmities of the tribes themselves. . . . We stand here today as if upon the ruins of a fallen race, to revive reminiscences of the past, and . . . to transmit them down to the far-off coming generations. . . . This, of all others, was the primeval standpoint from which the wild forest of New England began to discard its barbarisms . . . [and from which the] devastating inroads made by barbarous Indians in this then wilderness, began to yield to the progress of Pilgrim settlers, and to the transcendent march of civilization in a new world.[30]

Five years later another statue of Hannah Duston was erected in Haverhill, in a prominent downtown location. While the right hand of this figure again grips a tomahawk, the extended left hand is empty, and seems to point a finger of judgment downward toward unseen enemies lying at the heroine's feet.

The markedly different representation of Duston in the Haverhill monument seems instructive. With a tomahawk in her right hand and nothing in her left, we may see Duston unambiguously as an innocent captive, taking bold and righteous action to free herself and others. Commenting on the nation's fascination with the Hannah Duston story during the nineteenth century, contemporary historian Barbara Cutter sees the evolution of this narrative against the backdrop of a prevalent "gendered notion that men were more violent than women." She argues that the Duston story is one of the many "feminized representations of the nation [that] worked to create a model of American identity in which violence committed by the United States was, by definition, feminine, and therefore innocent, defensive violence." Cutter concludes that, by connecting "female virtue" with the nation's character, the Duston story furthered the development of a "gendered ideology of American innocence."[31]

To say the least, Hannah Duston is a rather complicated emblem of a city's life. Despite the fact that she is at once a tragic and violent figure, various local institutions are named after her, including a school and a nursing home. In 2006 her image became prominent once again when a local arts group borrowed and altered a photo of the Haverhill statue for a poster advertising a rock music event called "Battle of the Bands." The image eliminated the tomahawk and placed an electric guitar in Duston's hands. This clever bit of PR set off a wave of local, and wider, controversy about the use of Duston's image in this vein. Whether the main offense was irreverence toward a local heroine or casual use of an image of brutal violence was hard to tell. In a letter to the local newspaper, a representative of the

Abenaki tribe took the opportunity of the poster controversy to make the case that the settlers' version of the Duston story willfully misinterpreted Native American culture (including the practice of taking captives) to justify the colonists' act of revenge.[32]

While historians—at academic institutions and local historical societies—know and reflect on place-based narratives like the Hannah Duston story, such narratives are rarely used as a serious resource for either congregational development or civic reflection. I want to suggest that a whole new category of outreach or community ministry or *tikkun olam* (Hebrew for "healing the world") is waiting to be created by congregations bold and imaginative enough to become narrative leaders within their civic contexts. Such congregations would ask themselves:

+ How do powerful place-based narratives (like the Hannah Duston story) shape the soul of a community?
+ How is the impact of these narratives visible in the community's present-day character and self-perception?
+ How does the story of our own congregation weave its way through the narrative of our community? Who or what have we been to this place in the past, and who are we to this place today?
+ What kinds of dialogue might allow community residents to reexplore the meaning of place-based narratives from multiple viewpoints, with minimal defensiveness about problematic aspects of the story?
+ And how might a congregation use place-based narratives as an entry point for redemptive interaction with the soul of the place it inhabits?

Questions like these have the potential to generate innovative forms of missional engagement between congregation and community. A whole new field of practice is waiting to be created.

## Planting Seeds for a Field of Practice

For the past two years I have been considering *how* narrative leadership could generate a new and distinctive form of
missional engagement of congregations with their communities. I have been pursuing these questions from a peculiar
standpoint—that of a citizen and community leader who is
also person of faith, a local congregant, and a consultant to congregations all over the country. Stating it that way may seem
like an odd reversal of my credentials for this work, given that
my career has evolved almost entirely *inside* congregations and
church-related institutions. But during my summer sabbatical
in 2005, the fundamental orientation of my consciousness re-
versed itself, "changing polarity" rather suddenly, as the earth's
magnetic field is thought to have done at certain points in our
planetary past. Since then, my most generative standpoint for
imagining new missional possibilities for congregations has
been located on the *community* side of the church-community
boundary.

Because of one-to-one contacts I had made with local
community leaders during my sabbatical, I was invited at the
end of that summer to join a core group of fifty people drawn
from all segments of the city's life, including government, business, nonprofit organizations, faith communities, and newer
residents (this last being the slot I was asked to fill). Dubbed
"Team Haverhill," this core group had been called together by
a local foundation allied with the Chamber of Commerce to
generate a community vision for our city, guided by an outside
consultant they had engaged for this purpose. Over a period
of nine months, the consultant organized about twenty community focus groups, guided a dozen task forces as they explored specific areas for action, and facilitated the whole group
in development of a rough strategic plan. After some painful
struggles to establish a workable identity and structure, Team

Haverhill emerged as an independent, nonpartisan citizen-action group, and I have served on its leadership team since January 2007. Results achieved since the group's inception include installing twenty locally themed murals downtown; renovating three public recreation areas; cosponsoring mayoral candidate debates during two electoral cycles; successfully advocating expanded curbside recycling; revitalizing a nearly defunct Farmers' Market operation; and incubating a major partnership among four youth-serving agencies and the public schools, designed to coordinate and expand opportunities for youngsters to be mentored by well-prepared and well-supervised community volunteers.

Over the past year, involvement with this community group has provided me with an opportunity to experiment with place-based narratives. One of Team Haverhill's newest initiatives is an annual three-month public art installation called "Soles of Haverhill," modeled on communities all around the country that select an iconic animal or object as a symbol of place; mass-produce a large fiberglass sculpture of this object; invite a wide range of artists to embellish the surface of the forms in creative ways; display the artworks in prominent public locations during a festival period; then auction off the sculptures to support arts, culture, and community service organizations. Examples include the "Trail of the Painted Ponies" in Santa Fe, New Mexico, and the "Moose Parade" throughout the state of New Hampshire. Haverhill's iconic object is a lady's high-button shoe—a product for which Haverhill was once quite famous around the world.

The development, flourishing, and demise of the shoe industry constitutes a place-based narrative of great significance for the city of Haverhill. Unlike the distant and heavily mythologized Duston story, the shoe history of this city has not completely passed from the memory of living residents. Haverhill's last shoe manufacturer moved out of the city as recently as 1995. Our local Boys and Girls Club has conducted interviews with older residents who still have firsthand recollections of employment in the shoe industry.

Haverhill had begun to establish itself as a major center of shoe production by 1830. Growth accelerated with the completion in the early 1840s of rail service from Boston through Haverhill to Portland, Maine, and was further fueled by orders for army shoes during the Civil War. Both the shoe industry and the city's population continued to grow; between 1890 and 1920, Haverhill's population nearly doubled, largely due to the influx of French-Canadian and Irish, then central and southern European immigrants, whose labor was needed as the shoe industry continued to expand and mechanize. By the mid-1920s—even before the Great Depression—the shoe industry was beginning to decline in the face of competition from other parts of the country. After a resurgence in strength during World War II, and a few years of relative stability, a sharper decline began, fueled this time by competition not only from other parts of the country but also from other parts of the world. From its all-time peak of about two hundred shoe manufacturers, Haverhill would slide all the way to zero in 1995 with the buyout and departure of Allen Shoes.

As might be expected, a considerable part of the city's built environment was once devoted to shoe manufacturing, leather processing, and other related businesses. Recently, several of the vacant or under-utilized factory buildings in the downtown shoe district have been converted—or slated for conversion—into apartments and condominiums, under the rubric of "transit-oriented development." Shoe-era buildings with more elaborate facades facing on two main streets have become restaurants, specialty shops, and galleries, as the downtown struggles to establish a new cultural and economic identity. The "Soles of Haverhill" public art project is designed to contribute to the city's revitalization by bringing together long-time residents' living memory of the industry, the energy of a new downtown population dwelling in converted factory buildings, and the creativity of local artists, each of whom is partnered with a sponsoring business and a specific beneficiary organization to produce each sculpture. The launch of this project seemed to provide a prime moment to begin working with Haverhill's shoe-related narrative.

I am currently partnering with a variety of churches, service groups, and other institutions to convene informal conversations about the significance of Haverhill's shoe story. After providing a thumbnail sketch of the city's shoe history (much like the summary I have provided here), I ask participants to fill out a brief questionnaire, which is meant primarily as a discussion starter but also provides me with a record of individual responses.

The first survey question identifies what year, and at what age, the respondent arrived in Haverhill. Question two is a multiple-choice item documenting involvement with or awareness of Haverhill's shoe industry. Options range from "I worked in Haverhill's shoe industry," to "What shoe industry? (Not part of my awareness at all)."

Question three asks for observations about the legacy of the city's shoe history—how it has affected the character of the city we live in today—in four categories:

+ physically (architecture, landscape, environment)
+ economically
+ socially (demographics, social and political attitudes, intergroup relations)
+ emotionally (community self-image, self-confidence, tone)

And a final question explores how the whole story of the shoe industry might contain lessons for the community today about the opportunities and choices before us. People are asked to consider what past strengths or strategies we might emulate and what hazards we should avoid.

On the civic side, I will be arranging visits to service clubs, senior citizen residences, and other locations to share the survey and conduct conversations about the questions it raises. I will be doing the same thing with groups in several congregations—though with the congregations, I will begin by asking them to explore the congregation's relationship to the shoe story. For example, some of the industry's "leading men" were also important leaders and benefactors in certain local churches, while other congregations may have contained many shoe workers. At least one congregation in the city was actively involved, through its outspoken minister, in a famous shoe-workers' strike.

As the project moves ahead, I expect to convene several larger conversations that bring together participants from these different settings to review the responses we have received and continue to draw learnings about the impact of the shoe industry, both on the "soul of Haverhill" today and on the civic choices before us now. One result will be a series of local newspaper articles on the theme, "Shoes and the Soul of Haverhill."

While these conversations are being initiated from the community side of the congregation-community boundary, I would like to suggest that congregations themselves (alone or in partnership with other congregations and civic groups) could become initiators and sponsors of this type of narrative reflection and civic dialogue. Such sponsorship and facilitation would constitute one new and distinctive form of missional engagement with place, and would undoubtedly lead to further developments in this still-unformed field of practice.

## Notes

~

1. Wendell Berry, address, Northeast Organic Farmers Association (NOFA) conference, Amherst, MA, 1998.

2. U.S. Census Bureau, "People on the Move: Geographic Mobility, 1999–2000," in *Population Profile of the United States: 2000* (Internet Release), ch. 3; www.census.gov/population/www/popprofile/files/2000/chap03.pdf.

3. Pew Research Center, "American Mobility: Who Moves? Who Stays Put? Where's Home?" December 17, 2008; updated December 29, 2008; U.S. Census Bureau, "Residential Mover Rate in U.S. Is Lowest Since Census Bureau Began Tracking in 1948," news release, April 22, 2009.

4. The Saguaro Institute, "Harvard-Convened Group of Nationwide Leaders Release Plan for Rebuilding Community Ties," news release, December 2000, http//:www.bettertogether.org/aboutthereport.htm.

5. See *Generations: The History of America's Future, 1584 to 2069* by Neil Howe and William Strauss (Quill Press, 1990).

6. Timothy Beatley, *Native to Nowhere: Sustaining Home and Community in a Global Age* (Washington, DC: Island Press, 2004), 17.

7. John Paul Lederach, *The Moral Imagination: The Art and Soul of Building Peace* (New York: Oxford University Press, 2005), 107.

8. Lederach, 106.

9. Parker J. Palmer, *The Company of Strangers: Christians and the Renewal of America's Public Life* (New York: Crossroad, 1981), 22–23.

10. I have drawn upon the summary of some of these frameworks found in Anthony E. Healy, *The Postindustrial Promise: Vital Religious Community in the 21st Century* (Herndon, VA: Alban Institute, 2005), 108–12.

11. Robert D. Putnam, *Bowling Alone: The Collapse and Revival of American Community* (New York: Simon and Schuster, 2000).

12. Nancy T. Ammerman, "Connecting the Mainline Protestant Churches with Public Life," in *The Quiet Hand of God: Faith-Based Activism and the Public Role of Mainline Protestantism*, ed. Robert Wuthnow and John H. Evans (Berkeley: University of California Press, 2002), 131.

13. Healy, 112.

14. When the Percept Group consults with denominational bodies, it provides a package of background materials for interpreting regional demographics. This basic framework is drawn from Percept's supplementary material; the Lake Wobegon analogy is mine.

15. David A. Roozen, William McKinney, and Jackson W. Carroll, *Varieties of Religious Presence: Mission in Public Life* (New York: Pilgrim Press, 1984).

16. This summary is drawn from Ammerman et al, *Studying Congregations: A New Handbook* (Nashville: Abingdon Press, 1998), 100.

17. Penny Edgell Becker, *Congregations in Conflict: Cultural Models of Local Religious Life* (New York: Cambridge University Press, 1999); Arthur E. Farnsley II, N. J. Demerath III, Etan Diamond, Mary L. Mapes, and Elfriede Wedam, *Sacred Circles, Public Squares: The Multicentering of American Religion* (Bloomington: Indiana University Press, 2004).

18. Carl S. Dudley and Sally A. Johnson, *Energizing the Congregation: Images that Shape Your Church's Ministry* (Louisville: Westminster/John Knox, 1993).

19. Carl S. Dudley, *Effective Small Churches in the Twenty-first Century* (Nashville: Abingdon Press, 2003), 160. This book also identifies a sixth self-image of a "local" type, which Dudley calls "Intentional," 166.

20. Nancy Tatom Ammerman, *Congregation and Community* (New Brunswick, NJ: Rutgers University Press, 1997). See also the excellent guide for congregational discernment prepared by Nancy Ammerman and Carl Dudley for churches seeking to apply the research learnings: *Congregations in Transition: A Guide for Analyzing, Assessing, and Adapting in Changing Communities* (San Francisco: Jossey-Bass, 2002).

21. Nancy L. Eiesland, *A Particular Place: Urban Restructuring and Religious Ecology in a Southern Exurb* (New Brunswick, NJ: Rutgers University Press, 2000).

22. See James F. Hopewell, *Congregation: Stories and Structures* (Philadelphia: Fortress Press, 1987).

23. See Richard Slotkin, *Regeneration Through Violence: The Mythology of the American Frontier, 1600–1860* (Norman, OK: University of Oklahoma Press, 1973).

24. See an excellent discussion of culture as a toolkit in chapter 1 of *How We Seek God Together: Exploring Worship Style* by Linda J. Clark *et al* (Herndon, VA: Alban Institute, 2001). Stories are a key component of this toolkit.

25. Thomas Dresser, *It Happened in Haverhill*, (Haverhill, MA: privately printed booklet, 1996).

26. The sermon was entitled, "Humiliations followed by Deliverances," and was first published in 1697, the same year as the event it describes. This story was subsequently included in Mather's *Magnalia Christi Americana* (1702).

27. This entire discussion of the literary history of the Duston narrative is summarized from Robert D. Arner, "The Story of Hannah Duston: Cotton Mather to Thoreau," *American Transcendental Quarterly* 18 (1973): 19–23. Cited from the website "Hawthorne in Salem," http://www.hawthorneinsalem.org/page/11883/ (accessed November 4, 2007).

28. Ibid.

29. Slotkin, ch. 4.

30. Caverly's historical address is included in his book, *Heroism of Hannah Duston: Together with the Indian Wars of New England* (Boston: B. B. Russell, 1874), 389–91. Quotation drawn from a facsimile of these pages found on the website www.hawthorneinsalem. org (accessed November 4, 2007).

31. Barbara Cutter, "The Female Indian Killer Memorialized: Hannah Duston and the Nineteenth–Century Feminization of American Violence," *Journal of Women's History* 20, no. 2 (Summer 2008): 10–33. The quoted material comes from the article's abstract.

32. Margaret Bruchac, "Reconsidering Hannah Duston," published as an opinion column in the Lawrence *Eagle-Tribune*, August 27, 2006.

# CHAPTER 5

# Giants and Grasshoppers
## STORIES THAT FRAME CONGREGATIONAL ANXIETY

~

### SUSAN BEAUMONT

The people were anxious, and with good reason. The Is-
raelite faith community had lived in upheaval for years.
Under Moses's leadership, they had given birth to an entirely
new way of being community, and they had done so without a
permanent home. The journey was arduous, but they had been
faithful—more or less—and now they were standing on the
edge of a promised new beginning. All they had to do was step
in and claim the property as their own, but anxiety got the better of them. This final step seemed scarier than all of its pre-
decessors. Here was the promised land just within their reach.
What if they grasped at it but couldn't attain it? Worse yet,
what if they attained it and it turned out to be less than what
they had been dreaming of after all these years?

And so they did what any self-respecting community of faith
would do. They formed an ad hoc committee to study the issue.
Members of the committee (spies) conducted a preliminary assessment. The committee grew worried that Moses might push
the community at a faster pace than they were ready to go. As a
result, in framing its recommendation, the committee painted a
picture that was extreme and frightening. "This is not the right
community for us! The people who live here are giants and we

look like mere grasshoppers by comparison." Community leaders decided to heed the advice of the committee and made the decision to stay out; wandering in the wilderness looked more attractive than perishing at the hands of giants.

This story, liberally retold from Numbers 13, illustrates what communities of faith so often do in times of anxiety. A subset of the community crafts a story to hold their anxiety and to frame their understanding of the problem. Eventually the larger community adopts the story. Finally, the story begins to shape the destiny of the community. Israel's story was fine for temporarily stopping leadership efforts at moving ahead, but it became a self-fulfilling prophecy. The people actually bought into the story that they were tiny in comparison to the giants of Canaan and adopted it as their own, telling it and retelling it over the years. The limiting and fear-based nature of the story paralyzed the people and set them up for years of additional wilderness wandering.

Congregations today live in anxious times, every bit as troubling as the time that hosted the wandering Israelites. The ways in which their giants are described are mind-boggling: postmodernism, multigenerationalism, ethnic and cultural diversity, evolving theologies, worship wars, and ill-equipped leaders. According to Webster, *anxiety* is the apprehension and uneasiness of mind that people experience over an impending or anticipated ill. Anxiety surfaces when people doubt their capacity to cope with an impending threat.[1] The giants on the horizon of church life today are producing unprecedented levels of congregational anxiety.

The effects of anxiety on human thinking and behavior are both observable and predictable. In his book *Congregational Leadership in Anxious Times*, Peter Steinke describes the predictability of anxiety in three significant ways: anxiety has a repressive effect, an infectious effect, and a reactive effect. Anxiety represses human functioning by decreasing the capacity to learn, replacing curiosity with a demand for certainty and stiffening positions over and against one another. Anxiety is also contagious. It connects people. Let one or two people unleash their anxiety and before long its ripple effect in the congregation can be seen. Finally, anxiety has a reactive effect. People oversimplify; they become indecisive and unable to react.[2]

In my own practice with congregations, I have noted a predictable expression of the repression, infection, and reactivity Steinke describes. Anxious systems frame stories to contain and express their angst. When a series of events occurs within the life of the congregation that people need to make meaning out of, they tell a story about it. Meaning making is a simplifying and coping mechanism. When people craft a story about what has happened to them, they make assertions about the character, the significance, and the morality of the situation. Initially, they may tell a variety of stories about what happened, each with a different spin. Fairly quickly, a common folklore emerges about what happened and why it happened. Someone draws a permanent frame around the story, creating a sense of optimism or pessimism about the outcome, and the community owns the story. Ultimately the story becomes a self-fulfilling prophecy, shaping next steps taken and ultimately framing the congregation's future.

## The Stories We Tell

As a consultant to congregations, I am often called to work with churches that are stuck. Leaders are aware that something is holding the congregation back from achieving its full potential, but they cannot get a clear enough perspective to figure out what the problems might be. In most situations I find that the story the congregation is telling about being stuck contains the clues for getting unstuck. Once I hear congregation members tell a story about their situation, I can begin to help them understand how their own narrative scenarios keep them from moving ahead. Within the stories I have collected over the

years I have noted three problematic story types that often sit
at the heart of stuck congregations:

1. The story that illustrates where things went wrong in
   the past and how the congregation will never recover
   from that event
2. The story that illustrates a triumphant moment in the
   past, but memorializes that event in such a way that it
   limits the congregation's future
3. The story about being stuck in the present, casting the
   teller in a noble role and finding someone else to blame
   for the congregation's problems

Let's look at each of these story types in turn and examine
the ways in which the story limits the congregation's ability to
move forward. I begin with the story about what went wrong
in the past.

## Stories that Frame Past Problems

Plum Brook Church has been struggling for years with insuf-
ficient finances to support congregation programs and staff
salaries. Here is the story church members tell about their
problematic past.[3]

> Twelve years ago we had a pastor who insisted on splitting our church
> to start a new church. He encouraged seventy-five of our members
> to move across town and begin Cornerstone Church. That split really
> hurt us in the long run. They got the moneyed members and we got
> the good real estate. We've been having financial problems ever since
> then.

Many people know and tell the story, even people who were not
church members at the time of the so-called split. The story
appears in this form in the church's archives, having become an
official part of congregational lore. Notice how the congregation frames the decision to start a new church as a decision

imposed upon it. People telling the story express no pride in their church having birthed a new ministry. In fact, they speak of this as a church split, which is language typically used to describe what happens when a faction of a church moves away during conflict. The church Plum Brook planted is a thriving and vibrant faith community today. Instead of celebrating that fact, Plum Brook mourns it. This story has helped Plum Brook form and sustain a culture of scarcity.

Congregations like Plum Brook craft and retell their stories to handle the anxiety that was first triggered by the events of the story. Over time the story has taken on multiple levels of meaning, and the container of anxiety the story holds becomes larger and larger. At Plum Brook, members rarely speak about how they might raise new resources to grow the church, its ministries, or its staff team. Nearly all of their time is spent trying to figure out how to reduce expenses. The congregation talks continually about whether it can really afford a two-clergy staff team. And the more they worry about the money "giant," the more often they craft themselves as scarcity "grasshoppers."

In spinning its stories, a congregation makes meaning out of its environment. Thomas Boomershine, an international author and speaker on biblical narrative, says, "Story is a primary language of experience. Telling and listening to a story has the same structure as our experience. One of the ways we know each other is by telling our stories."[4] The ways in which stories are crafted reveal remarkable things about a community's value system, its point of view about itself, and its sense of how it will manage the future.

## Stories that Frame Past Success but Freeze the Future

In this next example, we will look at story of past triumph that a congregation tells in such a way that it actually limits the future.

Pilgrim Congregational Church is one hundred thirty years old and floundering. Like many older mainline Protestant churches, the congregation has lost its connectedness to the community and the culture. The congregation has been slow to change and attracts few people under age fifty into its weekly worship venue. An oft-repeated story at Pilgrim is a story about one of its faith heroes, a member by the name of Hannah Pierce. The early 1900s was a dark time in the church's history, and Hannah single-handedly saved the church from extinction. Pilgrim lost its pastor, unable to support his salary. Weekly worship services had fallen by the wayside and only a few names were left on the congregational rolls. The community was suffering from a terrible depression. Hannah, the story is told, loyally showed up to open the doors of the church building every Sunday morning and light the lamps, just in case someone might come to worship. Hannah also made certain that annual documents were filed to maintain the legal status of the church for a period of years when the church had, for all practical purposes, ceased to exist. As people tell Hannah's story, they emphasize her steadfastness, her loyalty, and her devotion to the congregation. The way the story is told suggests that Hannah single-handedly guided the church through this era until the church experienced mysterious revitalization and began growing again. Over time Hannah's character traits in the story have become the congregation's core values. When members retell the story, they instruct themselves in the values of the congregation: loyalty, steadfastness, undying optimism, and staying the course.

The pastor at Pilgrim Congregational decided to do some research on Hannah's story. When he looked into the archives he discovered something quite remarkable about Hannah. The next chapter of congregational history, which still includes Hannah, is a critical part of the story but one that is never told. The rebirth of the church apparently took place with the arrival of a new pastor who gave sacrificially of his own resources to generate new life. Remarkably, this pastor's name is rarely mentioned among church members. The church began to thrive and experience new vitality only after a few brave members, Hannah Pierce among them, voted to tear down the old church structure and create something totally new in the community.

Why doesn't Pilgrim Congregational tell this part of the story? It is rich with imagery, colorful characters, and bold decisions. But these are not values the congregation holds today. This is a congregation very comfortable with the status quo and they don't really want to change. And so the story they choose to tell is a story that casts the heroine in a role of survival through tenacity. Telling a story in which the hero keeps doing the same thing she has always done (showing up, lighting the lamps, and filing the reports) is safer. Telling the story over time has created and preserved a false history of the church, and it has also passed along deadly core values from one generation to the next, values that illustrate why the congregation is struggling to reinvent itself: Don't change anything; don't reach out in new ways. Just keep showing up and eventually your steadfastness and faithfulness will pay off in revitalization.

## Stories that Frame Congregational Nobility

Finally, let's examine a story about being stuck in the present and finding someone else to blame. The anxious congregation will often frame its story in such a way that the story promotes a noble sense of the congregation's own misguided or mistaken actions. Congregational stories rarely portray the congregation as needy or its members as fearful. The stories typically identify a villain and an issue that listeners would find worthy of a good church fight: protecting tradition, maintaining orthodoxy, or sheltering the resources of the church from being squandered.

St. Matthew's Church has been through confusing times. During the past eight years the congregation added 190 new members, but they lost 176 old members. A variety of factors can be identified to explain the church's turmoil. The community in which St. Matthew's is located is highly transient with families continually transferred in and out by industry. Five years ago the leadership at St. Matthew's began experimenting with new forms of worship and new expressions of spirituality that have attracted many new members but have alienated many long-standing members. A much-loved pastor retired four years ago. Two years ago the current teaching pastor began to experience a profound personal change in his own theology, which he has openly expressed to the congregation in his weekly messages. This pastor is respected as an intellectual leader but is not a particularly strong personal care provider. Those over age sixty seem to dislike this pastor, and they feel he does not provide adequate pastoral care. St. Matthew's is obviously in turmoil. This is how the discontented members of the congregation are shaping their anxiety story.

> Our congregation is in conflict over theology. Pastor is taking us in theological directions that are dangerous. Over the past twelve weeks we have counted the times pastor has mentioned Jesus in a sermon. Jesus only showed up twice. Are we Christians or aren't we? Last month Helen came by the church to pick up her oldest daughter from confirmation class. She arrived early and sat quietly in the back of the parlor as the class was finishing. Toward the end of class one of the kids raised his hand to ask the pastor how he could justify belief in God with so much evil at work in the world. The pastor responded that there are lots of days he doesn't even believe in God. This was the last straw for Helen and the rest of us. We can't be part of a church that isn't going to teach the basic Christian tenets of the faith to its youth. We have a responsibility to protect the basic orthodoxy of our faith. The new people in this place don't even know what it means to be Lutheran.

Notice how the story of the disenfranchised members at St. Matthew's casts the teller in the hero role and the pastor as villain. The tellers are protectors of the tradition and orthodoxy. They feel justified in their anxiety because their cause is noble. The pastor's version of what transpired in the confirmation class is considerably different from this account, but that doesn't really matter. What matters is the story that has been crafted and repeated throughout the congregation because that story is shaping the congregation's perception and experience of truth.

As I worked with St. Matthew's, it became increasingly clear to me that the congregation was not conflicted about theology or doctrine. In careful dialogue circles set up to explore doctrine and theology, people demonstrated remarkable openness to a diversity of opinions and much more consensus of thought than had been suspected. What did become clear is that people felt very uncared for by their pastor. They did not relate to their pastor and didn't believe that he was good at reading people's anxiety level when he pushed them theologically. Why didn't they craft their anxiety story to include these truths? Because the full story doesn't have a neat outcome and it doesn't cast them in a noble light. They preferred seeing themselves as defenders of theological truth rather than seeing themselves as people who needed better care from their pastor. Unfortunately, the story that St. Matthew's is telling doesn't allow people to address the root causes of their concern. Instead, their story, and their thinking that their theological differences are irreconcilable, is leading them toward a church split.

Anxious congregations often fall into a harmful trap when making meaning out of their current circumstances. In the midst of their anxiety, they reduce very complex circumstances into a few easily articulated issues. Anxiety is almost always systemic, involving a myriad of issues. Perhaps the congregation is struggling with moving across a size growth barrier, changing demographics within its community, different generational preferences in worship, and confusion about its mission identity. Anxiety prevents members from grasping the full complexity of the situation. Instead, members look for a simple "they are giants" and "we are grasshoppers" story to manage their angst.

Unfortunately, and often dangerously, congregations tend to focus their anxiety on the person of the pastor. The pastor becomes the problem because a discussion about leadership effectiveness is something that congregations can understand and make meaning out of. They have language for that discussion. The systemic nature of all their other challenges is too complex to grapple with. Replacing a pastor is a much easier outcome to the story than working their way through the complexity of the issues that face them.

# Story Listening

Listening to the stories a congregation tells itself about its history, its heritage, its proudest moments and its sorriest moments can help surface and articulate core values that may be preventing the church from moving into a more positive future. Posing questions to a congregation to help verbalize the stories that are currently being formed about its experience can also surface the helpful and hurtful issues that frame people's perceptions. The following questions, posed within a safe story-telling environment, can invite a congregation to become more conscious of its own story line.

1.  Reflecting on your entire experience at _____ congregation, tell about a time when you felt the most engaged, alive, and motivated. Who was involved? What did you do? How did it feel?
2.  Tell about a time when you were most proud of your association with this congregation.
3.  Tell about a time when you felt sorry about something the congregation did.
4.  In everything that has led up to this moment in the life of the congregation, what is at the heart of the matter for you?

The first two questions are appreciative in nature and are informed by the discipline of appreciative inquiry. As people describe their proudest moments, they tend to place themselves within the story, reflecting upon their competence and strength.[5] The third question invites them to reflect upon their place within a sorrier moment. When framed in this way, the question generally prevents blaming and shaming and invites the storyteller to reflect upon his or her own role in that moment of regret. The final question allows the speaker to craft a story about the present anxiety. Generally, the stories that are told in response to this question reveal important clues about how a congregation is limiting itself, its thinking, and its response to current anxiety-producing circumstances.

As people respond to these questions, they reveal their story journey and the ways in which they make meaning out of congregational experience. Collectively, these four questions invite the telling of stories that contain rich references to the values people hold dear and the heroes they admire. These stories also contain the seeds of current discontent. Within a congregation's best and worst moments are clues to what people long for in their current experience: unmet needs, lost values, memories of a less anxious time.

A congregational leader might pose these questions to members of the congregation within the safety of a one-on-one interview. People are generally eager to share stories and impressions when they feel that someone is genuinely interested in their perspective. It can also be invigorating for the congregation as a whole to engage in group storytelling. People are delighted to share their stories within the context of a small group and to listen to the stories of others. I often find that group storytelling sessions result in newly forged relationships as people connect with the story of another. At First Church the pastor reported a remarkably different feel in worship on the Sunday following the storytelling and listening session. People moved to sit in different pews to be closer to new friends. A warmer spirit of hospitality filled the sanctuary as previous strangers greeted one another with a newfound sense of familiarity. When we hold the story that another has shared with us, we hold onto something sacred and holy. Sharing your own story and receiving the story of another is an exercise in sacred trust.

Should you decide to host a group storytelling session to help your congregation articulate its narrative theme, follow these simple steps:

1. Brief everyone in the room on the importance of honesty, speaking the truth, and honoring the truth shared by another.

2. Invite each participant to pair up with someone else they do not know well and who, on the surface, appears to be quite unlike them.

3. Direct each partnership to find a relatively quiet space to work for thirty to forty-five minutes. Then have each person interview his or her partner using the four questions posed earlier, taking careful notes to record the stories that are shared.

4. Next, direct each partnership to join with two other partnerships in the room to form a group of six people. Every person in the group selects one of his or her partner's stories and shares it with the group of six, telling the story in the first person, as if it were his or her own story.

5. After each member of the group has shared a story in the first person, the group reflects on the common themes and values that were contained within the collective stories. These themes and values are written on a flipchart and shared with the larger group.

6. Next, the facilitator hosts a large-group conversation about thematic elements that emerged and ways in

which those themes empower or restrict the ministry of the congregation.

Note that this exercise is not appropriate for a group that is experiencing high levels of conflict. A certain level of trust must be present in order for genuine storytelling to emerge. In a highly conflicted environment, the facilitator will want to conduct one-on-one storytelling interviews in place of the group experience.

At the conclusion of this exercise, the facilitator has a rich collection of story themes and values to use in crafting a leadership narrative. Once the stories have been assembled the leader can begin to do the following:

+ Articulate the collective story that the congregation tells about its past and present.
+ Identify the core values of the congregation and hold them up to scrutiny. Are these really the values that the congregation wants to embrace moving forward?
+ Identify problematic or limiting organizational themes that need to be reframed.
+ Pinpoint inaccuracies and factual errors that prevent the story from teaching its genuine message.

If congregations are to thrive in the midst of chaos and change, then congregation members must become intentional about telling better stories. They need to become more conscious about how they have scripted their giants and grasshoppers. Congregations need to identify the ways in which the stories they tell are limiting their potential. Congregational leaders must become more adept at listening to, articulating, and reframing truthful stories that lead the congregation toward a fuller existence and ministry.

Let us turn our attention to another biblical story, a story also told during a time of high anxiety in the Christian tradition. A small group of women visit a tomb on Easter morning, expecting to anoint the dead body of one they had hoped would be their Messiah. The tomb is empty. From this anxious experience, a story could be crafted in any number of ways. The story that has emerged is a story of resurrection and new life. It is a story that has changed and is changing the world. Christians are story people, people of The Book. The story that stands at the center of the Christian tradition is a story of resurrection, redemption, and hope. The stories that congregations and their leaders tell about themselves ought to reflect the seeds of hope and possibility born from that singular, remarkable story. The tomb is empty and Christ is risen, risen indeed!

## NOTES

1. *Webster's New Collegiate Dictionary*, 10th ed., s.v. "Anxiety."

2. Peter L. Steinke, *Congregational Leadership in Anxious Times: Being Calm and Courageous No Matter What* (Herndon, VA: Alban Institute, 2006), 7–14.

3. All of the congregations cited within this article are fictionalized. The stories are real stories gathered from my consulting practice, but names and key events in the stories have been changed to protect congregational identity.

4. Thomas E. Boomershine, *Story Journey: An Invitation to the Gospel as Storytelling* (Nashville: Abingdon Press, 1988), 18.

5. Appreciative inquiry is the study and exploration of what gives life to human systems when they function at their best. For a fuller understanding of appreciative inquiry, its origins and use, the reader can turn to *The Appreciative Inquiry Handbook* by David L. Cooperrider, Diana Whitney, and Jacqueline Stavros (San Francisco: Berrett-Koehler, 2005).

# CHAPTER 6

# Congregational Resilience, Conflict, and Narrative Approaches

~

## SUSAN NIENABER

During times of radical change or conflict, some communities and institutions find inner resources that allow them to face the turmoil with creativity and hope. I call these inner resources for growth during conflict "resilience." In my years of consulting with congregations, I have come to believe these resources of resilience are best identified through narrative processes.

This chapter explores several questions about congregations I have assisted and studied over the last few years. How do narratives work in one's own life, and what does this tell us about their power to transform? How does the approach of narrative theory, as described by Michael White and David Epston in *Narrative Means to Therapeutic Ends*,[1] inform the practice of congregational consulting, especially as congregations face conflict with resilience? How does this approach inform the kinds of interventions I use in the midst of conflict? What is the impact of a narrative theory on congregational systems and members? To what degree does a narrative approach increase congregational resilience to face conflict creatively?

The approach of narrative theory is especially helpful to my work as a counselor and as a consultant with congregations in transition.[2] As a licensed marriage and family therapist, I have found a narrative approach a useful, nonblaming, and more positive way to assist my clients as they seek to reauthor and restory their lives. As a consultant for the Alban Institute, I have found this approach equally useful to congregations in the face of conflict or change.

A hallmark of narrative theory, according to author and therapist Alice Morgan, is that it "views problems as separate from people and assumes that people have many skills, competencies, beliefs, values, commitments and abilities that will assist them to reduce the influence of problems in their lives."[3] In the end, narrative theory—as applied to congregations in conflict—helps them create an open environment of multiple versions of past and present stories, with the ear toward hearing the Spirit's call to be led toward a new future.

## How Narratives Shape Identity
## Reflecting on One's Own Story

Let me begin with a personal story to illustrate some of the most important aspects of narrative theory: identifying a healthy story, reinforcing it with thick description, and cocreating that story with input from others.

I enjoy being a Minnesotan. From our ten thousand lakes to our colorful politicians, like Jesse Ventura; from the self-effacing humor of Garrison Keillor to our shy Scandinavian Lutherans; and our public values of recycling and protecting the environment—I love Minnesota. One of my favorite things to do (when it's not snowing!) is gardening. While my neighbor is *master gardener*, I have come to accept that I am a *pretty good* gardener. I know the difference between a sugar maple and an

Acer ginnala maple. I like Grapette daylilies better than Stella de Oro. I know when to fertilize, approximately how much to water, and where to position most plants. I am a pretty good gardener.

I have constructed a particular story about myself as a Minnesota gardener who is pretty good. I have linked events from my experience as a gardener, consciously and unconsciously, in a constructive sequence over time, and I have attached meanings to these experiences. It is a positive story, and these beliefs give me energy to continue enjoying my hobby. This story contributes to my identity, self-esteem, and self-concept, which are shaped by multiple stories: as wife, mother, senior consultant, and pretty good Minnesota gardener.

In a narrative approach, as therapist and client work together to select more and more events to create a dominant plot, the story "gains richness and thickness."[4] Richness, for me, means that I now have examples of my gardening that show all the various facets of my experience—I am good with perennials, annuals, and container gardening. By thickness, I mean that, over time, I continue to add more examples of how I am a pretty good gardener, thus reinforcing the dominant story I want to claim. Clearly, I have elevated many positive experiences of my gardening and added significant meaning to them. By contrast, I choose not to include other more negative experiences of my gardening in my story. For example, I don't share the time one fall when I forgot to dig up some bulbs a friend had given me that had been in her family for generations, and so they were lost to the snows. Even in the midst of unflattering experiences, I still see myself as a pretty good gardener.

The reason I probably continue seeing myself as a pretty good gardener in spite of my many mistakes is that other people have made positive comments over the years about the beauty of my yard. Stories, you see, neither are created by oneself nor exist in isolation. They are *cocreated in relationship* with others who either share many of these same meanings or who add information that a person uses to change or shift the story of her experience with herself and those around her. This cocreation of stories, in fact, is a primary source of my own resilience in claiming to be a pretty good gardener. By using narrative theory approaches in my own life, I have built and reinforced an identity as a pretty good gardener over the years.

## Narrative Dynamics in Congregational Life

Building on these basics of how I use ideas from narrative theory, let's explore how this narrative approach operates in congregational life. Unlike the story above, which is autobiographical, the other stories in this chapter are composites of several congregational narratives, with changed details to protect their actual identities. If one of these stories sounds familiar, it may be because conflict and resilience can look quite similar across religious organizations.

Let's begin with an all too common story: conflict over the pastor's leadership. In a typical congregation facing such conflict, multiple stories coexist in the same church, often uncomfortably: the woman whose husband died of cancer who is so grateful to the pastor for being there with her in this time of loss; the member of the governing board who saw the pastor become angry at a recent meeting and who believes this pastor frequently loses it over the smallest concerns; the member whose best friend attended the pastor's previous church and "knows" it went down the tubes under this pastor's leadership; and the family that attended the pastor's previous church and when they moved to the area, began attending this congregation because they loved the pastor. Finally, the poor member who just doesn't know what to believe because she has never had a bad experience with the pastor, but so many of her friends are unhappy. In the midst of all these stories is the pastor with his or her own beliefs about what has caused the recent conflict, about the strengths and weaknesses he or she brings to the church, and about what needs to happen next.

This example illustrates another tenet of narrative theory: that people live in the midst of many stories at the same time. Even within individuals, Morgan writes, "no single story can encapsulate or handle all the contingencies of life and no single story is free of ambiguity."[5] In situations of conflict, each person is tempted to believe that his or her version of the truth is the right one, which tends to make everyone intolerant of the views of others. The higher the level of conflict becomes, the more resistant each faction is to individual differences—even within its own group.[6]

Anais Nin, the writer and diarist, said, "We don't see things the way they are. We see things the way we are."[7] This is a fundamental assumption of my work, and of narrative theory. To embrace change, I must embrace humility by realizing that my truth is only one facet of the gemstone. This is not a way of minimizing or demeaning my experience or that of another, because I recognize that many other experiences and truths are out there. I try to always respect each person's experience. For example, in cases of abuse or misconduct in a congregation, I always begin by validating the experience of the person who has been injured and work with the congregational system through that perspective. In addition to being open to another's view of the truth, Margaret Wheatley, author and speaker, writes that we need "a willingness to be disturbed"—a "willingness to have our beliefs and ideas challenged by what others think."[8] We have to engage in real conversations with those who don't think as we do. This real conversation is not a discussion in the traditional ways we think of discussions. Real conversation is neither a debate nor listening to a series of monologues. We

can get to a place of real dialogue "if we remain curious about
what someone else sees and refrain from convincing them of
our interpretation, [then] we develop a richer view of what
might be going on."[9]

For most people, giving up or changing their beliefs is very
difficult. I am not speaking here as much about theological beliefs as I am the beliefs people develop about what is going on
around them. Those beliefs give us a sense of control and stability when things seem chaotic or frightening. When we are
anxious and grasping to regain a sense of balance, we tend to
look for simple solutions to complex problems. Most typical in
congregations is that a small number of people have the highest
percentage of firsthand information about issues that may be
causing conflict. They begin to shape the story of what is happening early on, sometimes in ways that lead to personalization
and blame.

Blaming others is one way of trying to reestablish a sense of
control by putting the problem on someone else. Consequently,
blaming most often comes from those feeling the greatest loss
of control. By *control*, I don't mean behavior that tries to control
someone else or the reexertion of power by those who once had
it in a congregation but no longer do. Instead, I mean a certain
level of existential control in a person's life that is critical to his
or her sense of well-being. I find that those who don't tolerate
ambiguity well or who are afraid, due to feeling that part of
their life may be out of control (because of health issues, family, or work problems), often are the most vulnerable to using
blame and the most resistant to giving up certain beliefs.

Over my nearly twenty years as a pastor, therapist, and
conflict specialist, I am convinced with Margaret Wheatley
that "we can't be creative if we refuse to be confused."[10] Deep
transformation can only occur when we let go of cherished assumptions and constructively hold together multiple versions,
experiences, and stories of what is happening around us. Until
I allow my version of the truth to dissolve or be challenged, I

will be unable to move from my polarized state. I will be unable to open myself to the transforming work of the Spirit.

## Collective Stories within a Broader Social Context

While individuals have stories about themselves or about what is happening around them, families and communities have collective stories rich with identity and meaning. Growing up, I lived near a family that had many children. They saw themselves as a flexible family and adapted by developing a high tolerance for spontaneity and low expectations for control. They were, in my estimation looking back, a healthy and well-functioning family, although the kids were sometimes frustrated that things didn't get done in time to meet certain deadlines.

Likewise, congregations have collective stories about themselves and their history. One congregation I worked with did a wonderful job examining the history of how God had been at work through it in the world and discerning its call and purpose. This particular congregation told many stories of how its purpose and call were embodied in the congregation's culture. I observed the ways in which all that it did was aligned with that purpose. No wonder they were a vibrant and vital congregation.

Other congregations tell similar stories of strength in times of distress, transition, or change. One congregation in the midst of a crisis said, "We plan on showing the world how a church can cope and recover from these things." Another church claimed, "We are no longer the problem church in our region." These are just two examples of the ways in which a conflicted congregation's story of its identity and its ways of coping manifest themselves. Other chapters in this book explore ways that narrative approaches help congregations live into a new, more hopeful story.

Congregations in conflict or in the midst of transition are often unaware of what is happening in the broader culture and do not realize how these conditions are affecting them and contributing to feelings of frustration and desperation. One way that a narrative approach helps congregations in transition is to remind them that their collective stories are influenced by larger cultural and social influences. A common example is the mainline Protestant congregation that in the 1950s or 1960s built a new church in a first ring suburb of a large urban area. The population of that suburb exploded and the congregation enjoyed the fruits of this demographic shift. In its glory days, the church offered something for all ages, worship attendance was high, and money was not an issue.

However, by the 1990s racial and economic diversity in the area increased as long-standing residents of the suburb were aging. The congregation watched as other churches in the area capitalized on this diversity and continued to grow while its membership plateaued and began to decline. Now members look back to the glory days and try to revive some of those same programs, and they seek a pastor in his or her thirties with young children and a spouse who will be active in the congregation. They decide to renovate the building, hoping that "if we build it, they will come," but all that does is leave them with a costly mortgage. None of these efforts stems the tide of loss. Out of desperation, various groups within this church begin to compete for dwindling resources. Members are exhausted, groups are in constant conflict regarding their demands and preferences, and their spiritual vitality wanes.

This story about how the changing demographics of a U.S. metropolitan area affect congregations goes a long way toward helping this particular congregation see that its experience is not isolated but actually a common one due to broader cultural shifts. Such a story of the broader world helps the congregation focus its energies in more constructive ways, and it increases self-esteem as members come to see that the decline isn't because they are inept, bad, or lacking in faith. How they respond to a new description of their situation and build a new story of resilience is perhaps the most important choice they can make.

# Narrative Practices
# of Resilient Congregations

In my work with and study of congregations that are resilient in conflict, I find the following narrative practices, adapted from Alice Morgan's book *What Is Narrative Therapy?* to be particularly helpful tools for shaping constructive interventions. This list is neither an exhaustive list of narrative interventions nor a description of all the tools I use in my work, but it does identify some helpful narrative resources for congregational leaders and consultants.

## Clearing Up Communication
## by Deconstructing Old Stories

When a crisis or conflict occurs in a congregation, the most important thing that leaders need to do is communicate well with members. Good communication, however, is one of the most difficult tasks, because leaders frequently become confused about what is appropriate to share, especially in conflicts that involve issues of confidentiality—like personnel changes. Leaders can also get drawn into the conflict themselves, becoming defensive and overly attached to a particular version of the truth. When people become agitated in conflict, especially in the absence of accurate information, rumors and misinformation increase.

I remember one instance when a member wanted to know if a new staff person actually caused another staff person to be fired. This troubled her because she had heard members of her women's fellowship group complaining that the new staff person *had* to be the reason the other staff person left because the termination occurred right after the new staff person arrived. Another common example is when a beloved ministry program ends shortly after a new pastor arrives. Usually, this ending was already in the works before the pastor came and is a case of unfortunate timing; but, in the absence of good or timely communication, the lack of information can lead to unhelpful conclusions and assumptions, which generate problematic stories.

Deconstructing such problem-saturated stories is an essential part of unraveling various levels of communication and interpretation. When conflict reaches a high level, a breakdown in trust can take place, followed by a high degree of suspicion. This often means that staff and lay leaders have lost credibility, so the use of a communication task force becomes key. This group is not meant to function as a public relations group by spinning out a particular, politically correct version of what is happening. They are there, instead, to provide effective communication, in part, by deconstructing problem-saturated stories. It is important that this deconstruction be done in small groups, say at a congregational supper, or in various men's, women's and youth groups in the church, because, no one person contains all of the information or knowledge needed to communicate well in a complex situation.

## Asking Questions

Asking questions strategically is essential in narrative approaches. However, no magical list of questions or book tells congregational leaders or members which questions to ask. Instead, asking good questions requires thinking on your feet to respond to the situations at hand. As Michael White, one of the founders of narrative therapy, writes, "The analogies that we employ determine our examination of the world."[11] Or as the pioneer of appreciative inquiry David Cooperrider would say, "Our questions are fateful. What we choose to focus on expands; attention gives life."[12] In the midst of congregational conflict, I generally do not ask questions that cause people to ruminate on problems to the point of losing a hopeful focus on the future. Instead, I ask and encourage questions that help people unravel different versions of events and clarify what matters most to them.

## Externalizing the Problem

Most organizations in conflict have plenty of low self-esteem and blame to go around. A number of techniques can help groups get some distance from the issues that are consuming them. In a narrative approach, participants can create a name for a problem and make it a separate entity, thereby externalizing it. By listening and asking the right questions, consultants and leaders can help uncover a metaphor that can capture the problem. What I find most powerful about metaphors is how they change as individuals and groups change. They can actually become a way to measure progress. Another great thing about metaphors is that they can easily be connected to biblical stories or other stories from a particular faith tradition.

For example, when I was in my twenties I entered a normal, twentysomething life transition. However, I didn't know then how normal this was, developmentally speaking. I was anxious and uncomfortable because my whole life felt up in the air. In the midst of this transition, I had an image one day of sitting in the middle of a staircase. I had no idea whether I was going up or down the stairs. The metaphor reflected well my feelings of frustration and despair, but as I lived with that image I also noticed other things about my situation: I was not alone on that staircase; others who loved and supported me were there; I didn't need to rush or prematurely pick a direction to move on the staircase; I knew that my direction would become clear

over time. Then one day a few months later, I noticed that I
didn't feel like I was on the stairs anymore.

Congregational members who are going through crisis or trauma often use metaphorical language like, "It feels
like a flood came through and washed away everything and
everyone in this church that meant something to me." Over
the years I have heard several stories from congregations that
went through fires. One pastor told me, "As we stood there, arm
in arm, crying and watching the church burn to the ground,
one of the members lamented that our church was being destroyed. Another member said, 'No, just the building was being
destroyed, not the church—not the people who make up the
heart and soul of this church.'" Metaphors and images are powerful ways of coping and constructing new realities.

## Listening for the Exception

One helpful tool in narrative intervention is noticing occurrenc-
es that stand outside the dominant, problem-saturated story—
times when the problem did not dominate or perhaps appear at
all. When this happens, it is useful for the consultant or leader
to follow a line of strategic questioning to learn why things were
different in this instance and what contributed to a more positive experience. At the time the problem appeared, perhaps it
didn't have as much of a negative influence on congregational
members who were involved or these people chose different
ways to respond. By listening for exceptions, congregations can
gain some distance from the problem-saturated story and recall
some of their own resources for alternative responses.

## Naming an Alternative Story

As people attain a level of emotional distance from the problem
and become empowered to develop more effective responses, a
different story gradually emerges. This is when the transforma-

tion becomes most noticeable. I recently was speaking with a pastor who shared with me some experiences from his former church. He said that congregation members had very high expectations for the worship services and for his preaching; he knew when he arrived that in the past congregational members had been in conflict with other pastors regarding their preaching. He was not surprised when the eventual criticism came his way. "I knew that I would someday receive complaints about my sermons, no matter how hard I worked to prepare. One day several members sent their representative to tell me that my sermons were not as good now as they had been in the past. I thanked him for that feedback and said that I would commit myself to working much harder. The truth of the matter is that I didn't really change a thing, but I think the fact that I didn't respond defensively made a huge difference in their perceptions of my sermons. The criticism stopped, and a new acceptance of my preaching settled in. Many of the former pastors felt threatened and hurt when members criticized their sermons and their defensive reactions contributed to battle lines being drawn."

## Re-membering Conversations

The term re-membering was originally coined by anthropologist Barbara Myerhoff in 1982 and was linked to narrative theory by Michael White in 1997. This concept has tremendous spiritual, emotional, and relational power for me and my work. The use of the term re-membering is not just about recollecting or being reminded. It involves congregations and their members deliberately choosing who and what from their past they would like to have present in their lives in order to support their growth, change, and transformation.[13]

When faced with problems, most of us are tempted to become more isolated and disconnected from important relationships in our lives. Re-membering is a way to strengthen our growth by linking together the new, alternative story with a support system. Significant members in a new story may be people alive or no longer living. They could be real or imaginary people from the present or the past. Stories from Scripture also can be acts of re-membering, as when churches draw on the great cloud of witnesses (Heb. 12:1) who have gone before them and who have shared the same faith journey. Significant members in a new story may also include animals, places, symbols, or objects. Re-membering conversations might also include important matriarchs or patriarchs from the congregation's past.

I remember a particularly difficult day years ago when I had one of my first training sessions in mediation. I was already a veteran psychotherapist and had great confidence in my skills, but I struggled this day to make the shift to the mediator role. Looking back, a number of other things were happening that negatively affected my ability to concentrate that day, including feeling a bit ill. I remember dragging myself home that night feeling discouraged. I soon found myself thinking about a psychiatrist who provided consultation for me in my therapy work. I adored this doctor, had a strong bond with him, and knew that he had great respect for me as a person and a therapist. I felt relieved and comforted re-membering him, imagining what he would be saying to me at that moment and realizing that he knew I was skillful even though I had had a day of feeling de-skilled.

Congregational leaders can ask members to reflect on several aspects of re-membering in order to develop or reinforce a new, healthy story.

+ Who would be least surprised to hear about this congregation's recovery and progress?
+ Who else would know the stories of strength and resilience from this congregation's past?
+ What people in Scripture would most resonate with your congregation's story of triumph over trials?

## Using Written Information and Videotape

Videotaping along with strategically chosen written information can be used effectively to create shifts in a congregation's experience of itself. Processing new information visually is an important way to solidify new learning. For example, one congregation's governing board was having a hard time working together constructively in the midst of a congregation-wide conflict. Members of the board were behaving badly, yelling at each other, talking over each other and making attempts to sabotage progress. One recommendation I made was for them to have a parliamentarian or process consultant present at all meetings. This person would help the group reflect on their process and write up notes about how the process unfolded at meetings. Knowing that someone was watching their interactions helped several board members relax and behave more constructively.

However, in this case, some board members also needed a more immediate solution. One day a board member was going to miss an important meeting; I suggested that the board might videotape the meeting so that the missing member could stay connected to the discussion. As you can imagine, the inappropriate behaviors immediately stopped when people knew there would be a visual record of how they behaved. They never experienced those kinds of problems again at a board meeting.

## Gathering for Rituals and Celebrations

The important rituals, traditions, and celebratory events of faith communities also serve the purpose of narrative intervention. Several churches in my study of resilient congregations spoke about anniversary celebrations and their importance in the midst of their recovery from a high level of conflict or trauma, and how much these events aided their recovery. These events gave them opportunities to re-member who they were, why they were together, and their larger call and purpose given by God.

To be effective, rituals and celebrations need to be well timed. To engage a healing ritual prematurely will only escalate conflict and frustration. It will not resonate with members of the congregation and will feel false or contrived. In addition, rituals, celebrations, and sermons are not platforms for people's positions. They should not be used to exploit the situation or as a way to spin out a particular version of the truth. Instead, they are meant to help the entire congregation realize the variety of stories in play, and re-member the people and communities that wish the best for them.

## Facing Turmoil with Creativity and Hope

Early in my therapy practice, I wrestled to articulate why my identity as a pastoral psychotherapist was so important to me. I needed a story to help me understand what made my work different from that of a secular therapist and why this was a calling for me. One day I had an image of a forest or jungle and reflected on how my clients sought me out when they were feeling lost or trapped in the overgrowth. After joining my clients in their jungle and helping them navigate their way through, many would reach a clearing, a place where the hard work of therapy would lessen a bit, giving them a break to breathe and reflect. As they continued to grow and progress, it was as if they reached a river. Once they stepped into the river, I was keenly aware that I had not been alone in the therapy office with them. I could feel God's presence and a sense of transcendence. Once they stepped into the river, they experienced a flow and a synchronicity. Things began to click and come together for them, things that were rewarding and that supported continued growth.

Conflict and trauma in congregations present challenging forests or even jungles to traverse. As leaders attempt to deal with a crisis, the multiple stories and versions of what is happening or has happened can make leaders feel like they are walking through woods filled with landmines. Narrative frameworks—like those derived from narrative theory—testify that strength, inner peace, and resilience come as leaders realize that they need not debate the different versions of what is happening or attempt to talk people out of their versions of the truth. The truth lies somewhere in the midst of all those stories, and it will surface as these stories are embraced in the congregation's overall story. Giving people safe opportunities to constructively share those multiple versions prayerfully and in a spirit of curiosity and openness creates clearings in the woods that can bring transformation. Congregations are capable of reaching these clearings, and eventually even stepping into the river, as they cooperate with the Spirit's leading to do things they never dreamed possible.

## NOTES

~

1. Michael White and David Epston, *Narrative Means to Therapeutic Ends* (W. W. Norton, 2000).

2. Ibid.

3. Alice Morgan, *What Is Narrative Therapy? An Easy-to-Read Introduction* (Adelaide, Australia: Dulwich Centre Publications, 2000), 2.

4. Ibid., 6.

5. Ibid., 8.

6. Speed B. Leas, *Moving Your Church through Conflict* (Herndon, VA: Alban Institute, 1985); pdf download at http://www.alban.org/bookdetails.aspx?id=3544.

7. Anais Nin, *Seduction of the Minotaur* (Athens, OH: Swallow Press, 1961), 124.

8. Margaret J. Wheatley, *Turning to One Another: Simple Conversations to Restore Hope to the Future* (Berrett-Koehler, 2002), 34.

9. Margaret J. Wheatley, *Finding Our Way: Leadership for an Uncertain Time* (Berrett-Koehler, 2007), 92.

10. Wheatley, *Turning to One Another*, 37.

11. White and Epston, *Narrative Means to Therapeutic Ends*, 5.

12. David Cooperrider and Michael Avital, eds. *Constructive Discourse and Human Organization*, vol. 1, *Advances in Appreciative Inquiry* (Oxford: Elsevier Science, 2004), 105.

13. Morgan, *What Is Narrative Therapy?* 77.

# Contributors

**Susan Beaumont** is a senior consultant with the Alban Institute. Susan's consulting work specializes in the unique dynamics of large congregations, with particular emphasis on staff team dynamics, strategic leadership, long-term planning, clergy transition, and size transition issues. Her work synthesizes the best of business practice with careful theological reflection. She is an ordained minister in the American Baptist Churches USA and the coauthor of *When Moses Meets Aaron*.

**Larry A. Golemon** is an ordained Presbyterian minister and a consultant and researcher in theological education. He coauthored *Educating Clergy: Teaching Practices and Pastoral Imagination*, the Carnegie Foundation study of seminiaries, and recently directed the Narrative Leadership project for the Alban Institute and the Ecumenical Project at Virginia Theological Seminary.

**Alice Mann** is a senior consultant with the Alban Institute. An Episcopal priest who has served six congregations, she is a nationally recognized consultant-trainer who has focused on growth strategies, leadership skills, strategic planning, spirituality, and congregational development. She is the author of *The In-Between Church, Can Our Church Live?*, *Raising the Roof, Holy Conversations*, and the video resource *What Size Should We Be?*, and is at work on a new book on community ministry to be published by the Alban Institute.

**Susan Nienaber** is a senior consultant with the Alban Institute. Susan has an extensive background in conflict and crisis management/intervention, mediation, systems theory, personnel issues, professional misconduct, leadership coaching, interpersonal dynamics, and communications skills and dialogue. She leads retreats and workshops for clergy and laity on a variety of subjects and is the co-trainer for the Minnesota Council of Churches' ecumenical clergy boundaries training.

**Lawrence Peers** is a senior consultant and seminar leader with the Alban Institute, with expertise in whole systems strategic planning, congregational growth and change, clergy coaching, and conflict management. He has also served on the adjunct faculty of Hartford Seminary. An ordained minister for over twenty years, Larry has served local congregations, worked as director of congregational growth and research at a national denominational office, and served on a Sustaining Pastoral Excellence Program within a middle judicatory. He has doctorates in congregational studies from Hartford Seminary and in organizational change from Pepperdine University, as well as specialized training in narrative therapy and appreciative inquiry.

**Gil Rendle** was for many years a senior consultant with the Alban Institute. A United Methodist clergyperson with fifteen years of parish experience, he is now senior consultant with the Texas Methodist Foundation's Institute for Clergy and Congregational Excellence. He also works as an independent consultant on issues of judicatory and national denominational change. He has authored several Alban books, including *Holy Conversations*, *Leading Change in the Congregation*, *The Multigenerational Congregation*, and *When Moses Meet Aaron*.